REVISE BTEC NATIONAL
Animal Management

REVISION WORKBOOK

Series Consultant: Harry Smith

Authors: Leila Oates and Laura Johnston

- -

A note from the publisher

While the publishers have made every attempt to ensure that advice on the qualification and its assessment is accurate, the official specification and associated assessment guidance materials are the only authoritative source of information and should always be referred to for definitive guidance.

This qualification is reviewed on a regular basis and may be updated in the future. Any such updates that affect the content of this Revision Workbook will be outlined at www.pearsonfe.co.uk/BTECchanges.

> **For the full range of Pearson revision titles across KS2, KS3, GCSE, Functional Skills, AS/A Level and BTEC visit:**
> www.pearsonschools.co.uk/revise

Published by Pearson Education Limited, 80 Strand, London, WC2R 0RL.

www.pearsonschoolsandfecolleges.co.uk

Copies of official specifications for all Pearson qualifications may be found on the website: qualifications.pearson.com

Text and illustrations © Pearson Education Ltd 2017
Typeset and illustrated by Kamae Design
Produced by Out of House Publishing
Cover illustration by Miriam Sturdee

The rights of Leila Oates and Laura Johnston to be identified as authors of this work have been asserted by them in accordance with the Copyright, Designs and Patents Act 1988.

First published 2017

20 19 18
10 9 8 7 6 5 4 3

British Library Cataloguing in Publication Data
A catalogue record for this book is available from the British Library

ISBN 978 1 292 14999 8

Printed in Slovakia by Neografia

Acknowledgements
The author and publisher would like to thank the following individuals and organisations for permission to reproduce photographs:

Shutterstock: 2630ben 38.

Notes from the publisher
1. While the publishers have made every attempt to ensure that advice on the qualification and its assessment is accurate, the official specification and associated assessment guidance materials are the only authoritative source of information and should always be referred to for definitive guidance.

Pearson examiners have not contributed to any sections in this resource relevant to examination papers for which they have responsibility.

2. Pearson has robust editorial processes, including answer and fact checks, to ensure the accuracy of the content in this publication, and every effort is made to ensure this publication is free of errors. We are, however, only human, and occasionally errors do occur. Pearson is not liable for any misunderstandings that arise as a result of errors in this publication, but it is our priority to ensure that the content is accurate. If you spot an error, please do contact us at resourcescorrections@pearson.com so we can make sure it is corrected.

Websites
Pearson Education Limited is not responsible for the content of any external internet sites. It is essential for tutors to preview each website before using it in class so as to ensure that the URL is still accurate, relevant and appropriate. We suggest that tutors bookmark useful websites and consider enabling students to access them through the school/college intranet.

Introduction

Which units should you revise?

This Workbook has been designed to help you revise the skills you may need for the externally assessed units of your course. Remember that you won't necessarily be studying all the units included here – it will depend on the qualification you are taking.

BTEC National qualification	Externally assessed units
Extended Certificate	Unit 3: Animal Welfare and Ethics
For both: Foundation Diploma Diploma	Unit 2: Animal Biology Unit 3: Animal Welfare and Ethics
Extended Diploma with Science	Unit 1: Animal Breeding and Genetics Unit 2: Animal Biology Unit 3: Animal Welfare and Ethics

Your Workbook

Each unit in this Workbook contains either one or two sets of revision questions or revision tasks to help you **revise the skills** you may need in your assessment. The selected content, outcomes, questions and answers used in each unit are provided to help you to revise content and ways of applying your skills. Ask your tutor or check the Pearson website for the most up-to-date **Sample Assessment Material** and **Mark Schemes** to get an indication of the structure of your actual assessment and what this requires of you. The detail of the actual assessment may change, so always make sure you are up to date.

This Workbook will often include one or more useful features that explain or break down longer questions or tasks. Remember that these features won't appear in your actual assessment.

> Grey boxes like this contain **hints and tips** about ways that you might complete a task, interpret a brief, understand a concept or structure your responses.

 This icon will appear next to **an example partial answer** to a revision question or task. You should read the partial answer carefully, then complete it in your own words.

> This is a **revision activity**. It will help you understand some of the skills needed to complete the revision task or question.

> 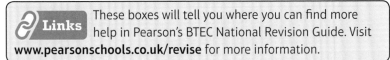 These boxes will tell you where you can find more help in Pearson's BTEC National Revision Guide. Visit **www.pearsonschools.co.uk/revise** for more information.

There is often space on the pages for you to write in. However, if you are carrying out research and making ongoing notes, you may want to use separate paper. Similarly, some units will be assessed through submission of digital files, or on screen, rather than on paper. Ask your tutor or check the Pearson website for the most up-to-date details.

Contents

Introduction

A small bit of small print

Pearson publishes Sample Assessment Material and the Specification on its website. This is the official content and this book should be used in conjunction with it. The questions and revision tasks in this book have been written to help you practise the knowledge and skills you will require for your assessment. Remember: the real assessment may not look like this.

Unit 1: Animal Breeding and Genetics

Your set task

Unit 1 will be assessed through a task, which will be set by Pearson. You will need to use your understanding of animal breeding and genetics, along with your own skills in carrying out research based on a set task brief you are given. You will then answer questions based on your research and your knowledge of animal breeding and genetics. These questions may require both short and long answers.

Your Revision Workbook

This Workbook is designed to **revise skills** that might be needed in your assessed task. The content, outcomes, questions and answers are provided to help you to revise content and ways of applying your skills. Ask your tutor or check the **Pearson website** for the most up-to-date **Sample Assessment Material** and **Mark Scheme** to get an indication of the structure of your assessed task and what this requires of you. Notice the example given in relation to the task given, the amount of time given for research and for the set task, as well as whether or not you may bring notes into the assessment. The details of the actual assessed task may change so always make sure you are up to date.

This Workbook contains two revision tasks to help you revise the skills that might be needed in your assessed task.

In this Workbook you will use your skills to:
- read and make notes on a provided scenario (pages 2 and 20)
- plan your time and how you will tackle your research (pages 3 and 21)
- carry out your own independent secondary research related to the scenario provided (pages 4–10 and 22–25)
- respond to long and short answer questions based on your knowledge of animal breeding and genetics and the task information provided (pages 11–19 and 26–34).

Your responses to the questions will help you to revise your skills and abilities to:
- demonstrate your knowledge and understanding of principles, practices, techniques and strategies related to animal breeding and genetics
- apply your knowledge and understanding of these principles, practices, techniques and strategies to realistic breeding scenarios
- analyse and evaluate information relating to animal breeding and genetics
- show that you know how to develop breeding management programmes and recommend breeding strategies in context with appropriate justification.

Links To help you revise skills that might be needed in your Unit 1 set task this Workbook contains two revision tasks starting on pages 2 and 20. The first is guided and models good techniques, to help you develop your skills. The second gives you the opportunity to apply the skills you have developed. See the introduction on page iii for more information on features included to help you revise.

Revision task 1

You need to make sure you use your research time wisely, by reading the brief carefully, planning how to use your time and making useful notes that will be helpful in answering the questions in your assessed task. Below you will find an example task brief and information to practise this. In your actual set task, you may be given guidance on the amount of time available for research and whether you are able to take your notes into the assessment. Ask your tutor or check the Pearson website for the most up to date Sample Assessment Material and Mark Scheme to be clear what will be expected in the set task.

Task brief

You are required to carry out research into the scenario provided in the task information below. You should consider the following areas in relation to the scenario:
- the animal breeds and their breeding standards
- husbandry requirements, care plans and reproductive behaviours for those breeds.

Task information

Make sure you read the task brief and task information thoroughly. This will ensure that you:
- focus on the key points in the data and information
- produce accurate and useful notes
- don't waste valuable time doing things that are not connected to the tasks.

Remember: Although the task information is directing you to look at information specific to some cattle breeds, there could still be questions on any of the general topics you have learned about in this unit.

You have been asked by William Jones, the owner of a local smallholding, to provide information that can help produce an effective system for the breeding of beef cattle.

The smallholding operates as a working farm, which William wants to expand into beef cattle farming. He has already carried out some small-scale breeding, but this has not been very successful. He wants to put in place a better plan for breeding his cattle.

The cattle breeds that he is considering are:
- Aberdeen Angus
- Red Poll
- Hereford
- Limousin
- Dexter.

Your job is to advise William on breed standards, husbandry requirements, mating/reproductive behaviours, methods of controlling and detecting pregnancy, and neonatal care, so that he can put in place a more successful breeding programme.

Over the next pages, you will find guidance and support on how to respond to this task information, including how to plan your time, carry out your own preparatory research and making notes.

Plan your research

You may have a limited time to carry out your research. It is really important that you use your time wisely. By spending 10 minutes planning, you will ensure that you cover all the key points that you need to research and leave yourself enough time to make a good set of notes.

Complete the table below to ensure you are clear on the areas you need to research for this Revision task.

Stage	Done
Read the task information and identify which areas need further research.	☐
There are 5 cattle breeds. For each breed, investigate breed standards and make notes. Aberdeen Angus Red Poll Hereford Limousin Dexter	☐ ☐ ☐ ☐ ☐
Carry out further research on cattle and make notes on: • husbandry requirements • reproductive/mating behaviours • nutritional requirements • methods to control/detect pregnancy • neonatal care strategies.	☐ ☐ ☐ ☐ ☐
Identify any other unit content that I need to revise and make notes if needed.	☐
Put my notes together and check my notes are complete and easy for me to understand.	☐

In your actual assessment, you may not be allowed to refer to notes, or there may be restrictions on the length and type of notes that are allowed. Check with your tutor or look at the most up-to-date Sample Assessment Material on the Pearson website for information.

Research cattle breed information

In the task information, you are asked to advise the smallholder on breed standards for the cattle William is considering purchasing. In your first piece of research, therefore, you need to find out more about these breeds and make relevant notes.

There are many breeds of cattle in the UK. Each breed has a set of standard characteristics and animals of the breed are assessed against these standards. Complete the table below using your own research.

Cattle breeds

Breed	Standards
Dexter	Use: Meat and dairy Size: 300–400 kg Breeding: Extremely maternal, calving problems are rare. Heifers mature young and can be put to the bull at .... to .... months of age. Should breed regularly for .... years or more. Temperament: Variable temperament but usually docile if handled regularly. Economics: Can be grazed on less acreage – more economical. High yield of ...., ... beef. Society website: www.dextercattle.co.uk
Aberdeen Angus	Use: Meat Size: ....–850 kg Breeding: Extremely maternal (good ....), calving problems are rare. Females calve easily and have good calf-rearing ability. Temperament: Good natured, ..., ... Economics: Hardy, adaptable, can be grazed on .... acreage - .... economical. High yield of marbled beef. Society website: www.aberdeen-angus.co.uk
Red Poll	Use: Meat Size: .... – .... kg Breeding: ...., ... Temperament: .... Economics: Fatten readily, high quality beef. Society website: www.redpoll.org
Limousin	Use: .... Size: .... – .... kg Breeding: High conception rate, calving problems are rare, good milking ability. Temperament: Can be .... Economics: ...., ..., ... Society website: www.limousin.co.uk
Hereford	Use: Meat Size: .... – .... kg Breeding: ...., ... Temperament: .... Economics: .... Society website: www.herefordcattle.org

Research husbandry requirements of cattle

You should already be aware of the different husbandry requirements from studying Unit 1, but now you will need to focus on those requirements specific to cattle. Husbandry practices include: feeding, watering, dehorning, castrating, weaning, worming, vaccinating.

You could look back over your course notes and make notes of the key points, as well as carrying out more research that may be relevant to the task information you have been given. Complete the notes started for you below.

Husbandry requirements of cattle

Feeding: ....

....

Watering: fresh water should be available at all times.

Dehorning: before calves are .... months old, using a .... iron.

Castration: A permitted procedure in cattle (Mutilations (Permitted Procedures) (England) Regulations, 2007). Under the .... Act (1966), only a veterinary surgeon may castrate a calf which has reached the age of two months.

- **Surgical**: Anaesthetic must be administered in animals of two months or more.

- Only .... are allowed to carry out this procedure.

- **Rubber ring**: Animal must not be more than .... days of age.

- **Burdizzo clamp**: .... must be administered in animals of two months or more.

Weaning: ....

....

Worming: ....

....

Vaccinations for beef cattle: ....

....

Other notes

You can make notes here of any information you have struggled to remember during the unit and think may be useful, such as processes and key terms.

....

....

....

....

....

....

....

Research reproductive/mating behaviours of cattle

You should already be aware of the mating behaviours from studying Unit 1, but now you will need to focus on those behaviours specific to cattle. You could look back over your course notes and make notes of the key points, as well as carry out more research that may be relevant to the task information you have been given.

How do cows indicate they are ready to mate? Is mating seasonal? You may already know some relevant information, but you should check your information is correct and complete. Complete the notes started for you below.

<u>Mating behaviours of cattle</u>

Mating strategy: in order to identify a suitable mate, cattle rely mostly on .... information.

Mating season: ....

....

....

Mating behaviours (female): Stand still to be mounted by cows and bulls, rubbing horns and grooming between animals is common.

Mating behaviours (male): ....

....

....

Other notes: ....

....

....

....

....

....

....

....

....

....

....

....

....

Links See page 17 of the Revision Guide to revise reproductive and mating behaviours of cattle.

Research methods of controlling/detecting pregnancy

You should already be aware of the methods of controlling and detecting pregnancy in cattle from studying Unit 1, but this is an opportunity to look back over your course notes and make notes to help you remember the key points, as well as carrying out more research that may be relevant to the task information you have been given.

Read the task information again, research and make notes on the methods of controlling/detecting pregnancy in cattle. Use the notes started for you below as a guide.

Controlling pregnancy in cattle

Hormonal: progesterone can be administered intravaginally or orally. This can be used to synchronise oestrous through controlling decay of the corpus luteum or ovulation.

> Add your own notes about other ways of controlling pregnancy in cattle.

....

....

....

....

Detecting pregnancy in cattle

Ultrasound scan: ....

Hormone test: ....

Rectal palpation: pregnant cows may show signs such as asymmetrical uterine horns, a prominent corpus luteum on the ovary, soft uterus and horn where the foetus is developing, palpable foetus. This is most accurate later in gestation.

None – return to oestrous: if the cow is not showing signs of oestrous three weeks after mating or artificial insemination, she is usually assumed to be gravid.

> Add your own notes about detecting pregnancy in cattle.

....

....

....

....

....

....

....

....

....

Links You can find some information about methods of controlling and detecting pregnancy in cattle on pages 19–20 of the Revision Guide.

You might also find the following book useful:

Gordon, I. (1983), *Controlled Breeding in Farm Animals*, Pergamon Press: Oxford

> 🖋 **Research nutritional requirements**
>
> You should research quantitative data about changes to nutritional requirements with breeding, including before, during and after gestation. Make sure you include information about all key nutrient groups. You can include tables in your notes – this would be a good way of showing this information concisely.

Before gestation: ....

....

....

....

....

....

....

....

During gestation: ....

....

....

....

....

....

....

....

After gestation an increase in nutrients is needed to allow for: ....

....

....

....

....

....

....

✎ Research neonatal care strategies

You should research information regarding neonatal care strategies for cattle. Make sure you include information on how neonates are cared for, how long this lasts and any adjustments that may be needed to the care of the herd.

Natural rearing system: calves are cared for maternally until weaning (which can occur anywhere from

....

Artificial rearing system: ....

....

....

By law (Welfare of Farmed Animals (England) Regulations 2007), calves must have received bovine

colostrum within ....

....

Calves and cows should be observed ....

....

....

....

....

....

....

....

....

....

....

....

....

....

....

....

....

....

....

See page 25 of the Revision Guide to remind yourself more about mammalian neonatal care strategies.

Identifying areas of weakness

As well as your preparatory research focused on the task information given, you should be revising all of the unit content. In your set task you may be asked questions about species or topics not directly related to the task information so it may be helpful to check you understand the wider subject content by auditing your knowledge and identifying areas to target.

Use the checklist below to identify any areas of animal breeding and genetics, especially in relation to the task information given, that you may need to create additional revision notes for.

Topic	I know this	More notes needed
Planning to breed: • Mate recognition strategy • Breeding value estimation • Inbreeding coefficients • Pedigrees • Selection differential • Intensity of selection • Response to selection • Non-random mating, positive assortative mating and negative assortative mating, outbreeding and inbreeding depression.	☐ ☐ ☐ ☐ ☐ ☐ ☐ ☐	☐ ☐ ☐ ☐ ☐ ☐ ☐ ☐
Animal evaluation and selection: • Behaviour/temperament • Body condition • Use of information resources, breed profiles, diagrams and images • Handling techniques • Use of equipment.	☐ ☐ ☐ ☐ ☐	☐ ☐ ☐ ☐ ☐
Management of breeding stock: • Nutritional requirements • Housing • Contraception and ovulation • Preparation for birth/hatching • Monitoring and common problems • Legal requirements.	☐ ☐ ☐ ☐ ☐ ☐	☐ ☐ ☐ ☐ ☐ ☐
Offspring: • Common problems and monitoring • Supportive measures • Monitoring systems • Hand-rearing.	☐ ☐ ☐ ☐	☐ ☐ ☐ ☐
Genetics: • Mendel's laws • Probability tests • Genetics diagrams e.g. Punnett squares • Gene interactions • Gene mutations • Genetic manipulation techniques • Stages in the process of genetic modification • Uses of gene manipulation in animal science • Commercial, social, practical and ethical implications of gene manipulation techniques.	☐ ☐ ☐ ☐ ☐ ☐ ☐ ☐ ☐	☐ ☐ ☐ ☐ ☐ ☐ ☐ ☐ ☐

In this revision task, you need to use the notes you have created on the previous pages, as well as your existing knowledge about Animal Breeding and Genetics to answer the questions given below.

Remember you will need to leave yourself enough time to answer all the questions, so don't spend too long on questions worth few marks.

Before you start answering the questions, remind yourself of the revision task brief and task information on page 2. In your actual assessment you will be provided with the task brief and the task information again.

Answer ALL questions. Write your answers in the spaces provided.

 1 Cattle have been kept as domestic animals in many countries for thousands of years. Many of the breeds available today were developed within the last few hundred years and not all of the historic breeds have survived.

(a) Give **two** survival strategies in cattle.

2 marks

Food availability, predation, disease resistance and economic value can all influence the survival of domestic animals.

Two survival strategies in cattle include their economic value as a source of food and resources

and ....

(b) Explain **three** factors which should be considered when evaluating the suitability of a bull for breeding.

6 marks

If you are asked to **explain** something, you need to make it clear, or state the reasons why it happens. You should not just give a list of reasons. You should include the things that will affect the ability of the animal to breed, its health and how easily it can be handled.

condition of mouth/teeth/eyes

head shape/size

markings/colour of skin/coat

desirable characteristics

size/condition of limbs

Factors affecting selection for breeding

horns

condition/formation of limbs/hooves/feet

previous breeding history

anus/cloaca/genitals

posture/conformation

....

....

....

....

....

....

....

....

....

....

....

....

> **Links** See pages 1 and 7–10 of the Revision Guide for more information about survival strategies and breeding in animals.

> **Guided** 2
>
> The yard manager wants to develop a new herd for beef production which will be put to graze in an exposed field. There are three small herds available for William to choose between.
>
> **Herd 1: Limousin**
> 3 cows, one calf and one proven bull. All TB clear and out on grass.
>
> **Herd 2: Dexter**
> 4 yearling heifers and one established cow with bull calf. All handled regularly. Worming and vaccines up-to-date.
>
> **Herd 3: Red Poll**
> 4 heifers aged 2 years. Very docile and easy to handle. TB clear.

> If you are asked to **assess**, you should include both the good and bad features.
>
> **Remember:** Exposed fields are susceptible to harsh weather conditions.

Assess the suitability of **each** herd for beef production. `12 marks`

> It might be useful to draw a table like the one below of the desirable characteristics and assess each herd against each characteristic. When writing your answer, you can refer to the positives and negatives you have identified. Consider the breed standards for each herd too in order to justify your choice.
>
> | Desirable characteristic | Herd | | |
> | --- | --- | --- | --- |
> | | Limousin | Dexter | Red Poll |
> | Fertility | | | |
> | Vaccinated | | | |
> | Temperament | | | |
> | Breeding | | | |

Limousin: generally hardy animals with a high conception rate and few breeding problems, making

them suitable for ....

....

....

....

....

....

....

....

....

....

....

....

....

....

....

....

....

....

....

....

....

....

....

....

....

....

....

....

....

....

....

....

....

Links You can find information about breeding programmes on pages 9–13 of the Revision Guide.

Guided ❯

3 William wants to increase the number of red Aberdeen Angus cattle. He is considering crossing a black Aberdeen Angus cow (XXBb) with a red Aberdeen Angus bull (XYbb).

(a) Calculate the phenotypic probability of producing a red heifer by using the dihybrid template provided.

4 marks

		Bull			
		Xb	Xb	Yb	Yb
Cow	XB	XXBb	XXBb	XYBb	XYBb
	XB				
	Xb				
	Xb				

<u>Phenotypic probability</u>

The probability that these parents will produce a red heifer is:

$\dfrac{}{16}$ = ...

> You could write this as a decimal, a percentage or a ratio.

(b) Identify **three** of Mendel's laws which are applied to these crosses.

3 marks

Law of independent ....

Law of ....

Law of ....

(c) Explain how DNA is linked to variation and evolution in cattle.

4 marks

> You need to think about how DNA can lead to variation and how this can lead to evolution, making sure you link this to the example of cattle. Things you may find it useful to consider include:
> • heredity   • mutation   • variation

....

....

....

....

....

....

....

....

....

....

> 🔗 **Links**   Look at pages 2–6 of the Revision Guide for more about genetics.

4 You are selecting a herd of cattle for meat production.

(a) Identify **four** things to consider when constructing a breeding programme.

4 marks

A successful breeding programme will be economically viable (growth rate, live birth rate, carcass yield) and involve suitable animals (genetics, temperament, health, conformation).

....

....

....

....

....

....

....

....

(b) Define the following terms: breeding value estimation, selection intensity and selection response.

3 marks

Breeding value estimation: how desirable an animal's genes are, as estimated from its phenotype.

Selection intensity: a measure of how .... an animal is to

....

Selection response: a prediction of ....

(c) Describe **three** ways in which selection and mating schemes in cattle can benefit humans.

3 marks

You should cover the effects on cost, productivity and uses.

Increased productivity increases ....

....

Increased product yield improves ....

....

Increased efficiency gives ....

....

(d) William wants to increase the value of the herd through selective breeding.
  Evaluate the features which could be encouraged to improve livestock breeds. `4 marks`

> For **evaluate** questions, you need to consider several options and come to a conclusion about their importance.
>
> To answer this question fully, you should identify what gives cattle their commercial value, and the advantages and disadvantages of breeding to promote these features.

....

....

....

....

....

....

....

....

> **Links** You can find more about the reasons for selective breeding on pages 7–8 of the Revision Guide.

Guided **5** | Pregnancy diagnosis is important to ensure that the correct care is provided for the cattle.

(a) Describe **two** devices and/or techniques which could be used for pregnancy diagnosis in cattle. `2 marks`

Visual signs such as ....

....

....

(b) Explain how hormone therapy, synchronisation and superovulation are used together in breeding cattle. `3 marks`

Hormone therapy is used in different ways in animal breeding. Firstly, hormone therapy can be

used to .... so that AI or mating can be carried out within

....

In addition, hormone therapy can also be used to encourage ....

....

> **Links** See page 18 of the Revision Guide for more information about hormone therapy, synchronisation and superovulation.

(c) William wants to ensure the herd are provided with a suitable diet. Explain how the nutritional requirements of the cattle should be monitored and adapted during gestation and throughout lactation.

4 marks

The nutritional requirements of cattle should be monitored by continually assessing the body score of the animals and the amounts of food consumed. During gestation, cattle need

> Monitoring an animal's condition often involves observing their behaviour and health.

....

....

....

....

....

....

....

(d) Good care of neonates is essential for healthy animals. Describe the care which should be given to a cow and its calf in the first 24 hours of life.

6 marks

> You should include information such as: how neonates are cared for, how long this lasts and adjustments needed to the care of the herd.

The cow and calf should be brought into a suitable shed or easy-to-monitor field prior to parturition. When the calf is born, ensure it is

> Continue this answer with your own ideas.

.... by its mother and breathing.

The umbilical cord should be coated in .... The cow and calf should remain somewhere

warm and ....

....

....

....

....

....

....

....

....

....

....

Guided **6** Genetic manipulation can be used to promote or reduce characteristics.

(a) Compare the advantages and disadvantages of genetic manipulation in the following areas: commercial, social, technological.

6 marks

What can be the benefits of genetic manipulation in each listed area? What can be the drawbacks?

Commercial advantages include the fact that animals can be produced which have a higher meat yield leading to increased commercial value.

Commercial disadvantages include ....

....

Social advantages such as ....

....

Social disadvantages can include ....

....

Tecnological advantages include ....

....

A technological disadvantage is the fact that ....

....

(b) Explain the impact of inbreeding on the health and value of the herd.

2 marks

Desirable traits can be encouraged, along with the expression of

.... genes.

You should include any positive and negative effects of inbreeding.

There is also potential for reduced ....

(c) Discuss **four** ethical issues faced by using genetic manipulation techniques in animals.

12 marks

Make sure you discuss four issues.

If you are asked to **discuss** something, you should state what the thing is and discuss how it is relevant.

The four ethical issues I am going to discuss are: animal welfare, potential impact on

non-modified organisms, environmental impact and ....

Animal welfare can be negatively affected by genetic manipulation, as the manipulations can cause welfare concerns, as with featherless chickens. However, the genetic manipulations can also treat problems such as genetic disorders.

There is the potential for the modified genes to impact on non-modified organisms in the food chain. Modifications could become widespread, causing changes for other animals in the area. Modifications could also be harmful to prey species.

Genetic manipulations could impact on the environment by ....

....

....

Now continue this answer, including at least one further issue. You could discuss religious concerns, animal rights or issues regulating the genetic manipulations.

....

....

....

....

....

....

....

....

....

....

....

....

....

....

Links See pages 36–37 of the Revision Guide for more information about the advantages, disadvantages and ethics of genetic manipulation.

END OF REVISION TASK

TOTAL FOR REVISION TASK = 80 MARKS

Revision task 2

 This task is less guided than the previous task. You will need to complete your research yourself and use it to answer the questions. Some hints are included to help prompt your answers.

Task brief

You are required to carry out research into the scenario provided in the task information below. You should consider the following areas in relation to the scenario:

- the animal breeds and their breeding standards
- husbandry requirements, care plans and reproductive behaviours for those breeds.

Task information

Make sure you read the task brief and task information thoroughly. This will help to ensure that you:
- fully understand what you have to do
- focus on the key points in the data and information
- produce the correct documents
- don't waste valuable time doing things that are not connected to the tasks
- maximise the opportunity to obtain marks.

George Black, a local dog breeder, has asked you to provide information to help him establish a sound approach to dog breeding. You will need to provide information on the following:

- breed standards for these domestic dog breeds:
  ◦ Labrador
  ◦ Siberian husky
  ◦ Springer spaniel
  ◦ Kuvasz
  ◦ Mexican hairless dog
- husbandry requirements, to include care plans
- reproductive/mating behaviours
- neonatal care
- common genetic problems
- relevant legislations.

Carry out your own research and make notes on each of the areas indicated in the task information:

- husbandry requirements for dogs – remember this can include cleaning, feeding, exercising and health measures

- mating behaviours in dogs

- reproductive behaviours in dogs

- neonatal care

- common genetic problems

- relevant laws for breeding dogs in the UK

- breed standards for:
  - Labrador
  - Siberian husky
  - Springer spaniel
  - Kuvasz
  - Mexican hairless dog.

You should find quantitative data about changes to nutritional requirements with breeding (including before, during and after gestation). Make sure you include information about all key nutrient groups. You can include tables in your notes – this would be a good way of showing this information concisely.

Remember: questions may not be limited to these topics. You could also be asked about genetic engineering techniques, ethics or any other topic you have learned about in Unit 1. You will need to revise these topics too and decide if you need to include any of these areas in your notes. See page 4 for a checklist to help you identify which areas you need to spend more time on.

....
....
....
....
....
....
....
....
....
....
....
....
....
....
....
....
....

> **Answer ALL questions. Write your answers in the spaces provided.**

> You will only have a limited time to answer all the questions in this section. Make sure you leave yourself enough time for each question, and remember that some questions are worth more marks than others.

1 Before developing a breeding programme, the owner has requested information about reproductive behaviours in dogs.

(a) Discuss how dogs use sensory information in mate recognition.   4 marks

> Sensory information can be auditory, somatosensory, gustatory, olfactory or visual.

....
....
....
....
....
....
....

> **Links** See page 17 of the Revision Guide for information about mate recognition systems in animals.

(b) Describe **four** things to consider when constructing a breeding programme for dogs.   4 marks

....
....
....
....
....
....

> **Links** See pages 9–13 of the Revision Guide for more information about constructing breeding programmes.

(c) Explain the neonatal care strategy used by dogs looking after their young.   2 marks

....
....
....

> **Links** To revise care plans for parturition and neonatal care for dogs, see page 25 of the Revision Guide.

(d) Discuss the changes to nutrition required by the bitch before gestation, during gestation and after parturition.　4 marks

> Structure your answer so that you cover the different stages in order – before, during and after parturition. The question asks about the bitch, so there is no need to discuss nutrition for puppies.

....

....

....

....

....

....

....

2 The breeder has a range of dogs of various breeds which could be used for breeding.

(a) State **four** factors which should be considered when evaluating the suitability of any animal for breeding.　4 marks

....

....

....

....

....

....

....

> **Links** Many factors contribute to whether an animal is suitable for breeding. You can find more information about this on page 10 of the Revision Guide.

(b) Describe the benefits of using pedigree animals in the breeding programme.　2 marks

> A **pedigree** is a record of the phenotypic background of an animal, its siblings, parents, grandparents and previous generations.

....

....

....

....

(c) Explain how calculating the inbreeding coefficient will help the breeder to select which animals to cross. `2 marks`

....

....

....

....

The breeder wants to ensure his dogs meet the requirements of many prospective dog owners.

(d) Explain **two** characteristics which could be encouraged in dogs intended as family pets and why these would be beneficial. `4 marks`

Think about desirable characteristics for the different roles that dogs have.

....

....

....

....

....

....

....

....

The breeder wants to increase the number of puppies he breeds that are able to act as guard dogs but still be suitable around young children.

(e) Assess the suitability of the following breeds for this: Siberian husky, Springer spaniel and Kuvasz. `6 marks`

....

....

....

....

....

....

....

....

....

....

....

....

....

3 In the past five years, the breeder's Siberian huskies have produced 28 huskies with amber eyes and 11 with blue eyes.

(a) Calculate the phenotypic ratio for this. Show your working.

2 marks

The **phenotypic probability** is the number of animals with a trait divided by the total number of animals.

Links To revise gene interactions and phenotypes, see pages 2–5 of the Revision Guide.

The breeder is considering purchasing a Siberian husky to use in the breeding programme. He has found two possible females available.

Female 1

Two-year-old bitch, not previously bred. No incidences of deformities for the previous four generations. Balanced conformation with an even temperament.

Female 2

Three-year-old bitch, one previous litter of six, all puppies survived and showed good conformation. Mild temperament and good conformation.

(b) Assess the suitability of the two animals described and advise the breeder which would be most suitable, providing reasons for your choice.

6 marks

....

....

....

....

....

....

....

....

....

....

....

(c) The breeder would like to visit both dogs to assess their suitability. Explain the features of a suitable body condition.

4 marks

Body condition scoring is a common technique used by breeders and pet owners to measure whether their animals are in good health, well cared for and fertile.

....

....

....

....

....

....

....

....

Links You can find more about the factors affecting selection for breeding on pages 10–13 of the Revision Guide.

4 | The dog breeder wants to increase the number of liver Labradors he has. Liver (bb) is recessive to black (B). Yellow (ee) masks the colours of both black and liver while the dominant allele does not mask the colours.

Mating female	Stud 1	Stud 2
Phenotype: yellow Labrador	**Phenotype:** black Labrador	**Phenotype:** black Labrador
Genotype: bbee	**Genotype:** BbEe	**Genotype:** BbEE

Calculate the dihybrid probabilities of offspring likely to be liver if the female is crossed with each of the males by using the dihybrid templates.

8 marks

The possible gene interactions are lethal alleles, incomplete dominance, co-dominance, epistatic effects, sex linkage, sex influenced or multiple alleles.

List the possible genotypes of the male along the top of the Punnett square, and the possible genotypes of the female along the left-hand side.

Stud 1			

Phenotypic probability = ...

Stud 2			

Phenotypic probability = ...

> **Links** There is more information about phenotypic ratios and probabilities on pages 3–4 of the Revision Guide.

5 There are currently over 340 recognised breeds of dog in the world.

(a) Describe how DNA mutations have led to this large number of breeds. 2 marks

Mutations can cause changes in the genotype and phenotype.

....

....

....

....

Mutations can have three types of effect on variation: harmful, beneficial and neutral.

(b) Explain the differences between these effects.　　2 marks

....

....

....

....

(c) Explain the difference between spontaneous and induced mutations.　　2 marks

....

....

....

....

Mexican Hairless, Peruvian Inca Orchid and Chinese Crested Dog are all heterozygous for dominant hairlessness. In these breeds, two copies of the dominant gene results in miscarriage or embryo reabsorption.

(d) Explain which type of genetic interaction this is and why it cannot be bred out.　　2 marks

The possible gene interactions are lethal alleles, incomplete dominance, co-dominance, epistatic effects, sex linkage, sex influenced or multiple alleles.

....

....

....

....

Links　See pages 6–7 of the Revision Guide for information on mutations.

6　The breeder has observed cherry eye, a hereditary condition, in one of his dogs.

(a) Explain how sequencing the genome of dogs could help identify causes of this.　　4 marks

....

....

....

....

....

....

....

....

(b) Describe the process of gene therapy.   4 marks

In gene therapy, techniques are used to make changes to the organism's genome.

....

....

....

....

....

....

....

....

Links To revise gene modification and gene therapy, see pages 33–34 of the Revision Guide.

The breeder is considering using cloning in some of the breeding programmes.

(c) Explain the advantages and disadvantages of cloning.   12 marks

In cloning, an exact copy of an organism is made.

....

....

....

....

....

....

....

....

....

....

....

....

....

....
....
....
....
....
....
....
....
....
....
....
....
....
....
....
....
....
....
....
....
....
....
....
....
....
....

Links See pages 32–36 of the Revision Guide for information on modifying genes.

END OF REVISION TASK

TOTAL FOR REVISION TASK = 80 MARKS

Unit 2: Animal Biology

Your exam

Unit 2 will be assessed through an exam, which will be set by Pearson. You will need to use your understanding of animal biology to respond to questions that require short and long answers.

Your Revision Workbook

This Workbook is designed to **revise skills** that might be needed in your exam. The selected content, outcomes, questions and answers are provided to help you to revise content and ways of applying your skills. Ask your tutor or check the **Pearson website** for the most up-to-date **Sample Assessment Material** and **Mark Scheme** to get an indication of the structure of your actual exam and what this requires of you. The details of the actual exam may change so always make sure you are up to date.

To support your revision, this Workbook contains revision questions to help you revise the skills that you might need in your exam. The maximum number of marks available for each question indicates the amount of time you should spend on that question.

These revision questions are divided into two sections:

Revision test 1

This is a revision test with additional guidance in the form of hints and guided answers to help you understand how to go about answering questions.

Revision test 2

This revision test has less guidance, to give you a chance to practise answering exam-type questions by yourself.

When in your exam, remember the following points.
- Use correct spelling, punctuation and grammar. Spelling is especially important for scientific vocabulary.
- Use a pen that writes in black ink, and make sure you have a spare pen with you.

> **Links** To help you revise skills that might be needed in your exam, this Workbook contains two sets of revision questions, starting on pages 36 and 43. The first is guided and models good techniques, to help you develop your skills. The second gives you the opportunity to apply the skills you have developed.
>
> See the introduction on page iii for more information on features included to help you revise.

Revision test 1

Answer ALL questions. Write your answers in the spaces provided.

 1 During the oestrous cycle the levels of hormones fluctuate. The table shows the measures of blood progesterone levels from five cows at the start of oestrous (Day 1) and later in the cycle (Day 16).

Progesterone levels (ng/ml)	Cow 1	Cow 2	Cow 3	Cow 4	Cow 5
Day 1	0.1	0.3	0.4	0.1	0.25
Day 16	4.7	6.0	5.2	3.2	4.9

Calculate the mean level of progesterone for:

(a) Day 1

0.1 + 0.3 + 0.4 + 0.1 + 0.25 = 1.15

1.15 ÷ 5 = ... ng/ml

1 mark

(b) Day 16

1 mark

....

....

Links See pages 89–91 of the Revision Guide for more information about hormone levels.

Guided **2** An animal cell is a cell in which all the organelles are contained in membranes. A typical animal cell is shown in the diagram below.

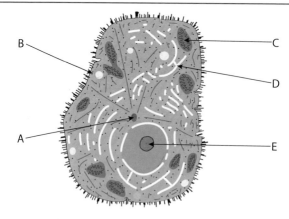

The possible answers include: endoplasmic reticulum, nucleolus, cytoplasm, mitochondrion, centriole.

(a) Give the names of the structures labelled A–E in the diagram.

5 marks

A Cytoskeleton ✗ ....

B Cytoplasm ✓ ....

C Mitrocondria ✓ ....

D Endoplasmic reticulum ✓ ....

E Nucleus ✓ ....

(b) Describe **three** functions of the plasma membrane. 3 marks

The plasma membrane .... what can

.... and leave the cell. It also allows cells to

.... to each other and ....

with each other.

> The cytoskeleton of a cell is made up of different fibres.

(c) State the **two** fibres associated with muscle contraction. 2 marks

> **State** questions require you to quickly recall facts or features.

The two fibres associated with muscle contraction are actin and ....

....

(d) Explain how the two fibres work together. 2 marks

> If you are asked to **explain** something, you need to make it clear, or state the reasons why it happens. You should not just give a list of reasons.

During muscle contraction, the two fibres ....

....

> **Links** See pages 46–47 of the Revision Guide for information about cellular ultrastructure, and pages 55 and 58 for information about muscle contraction.

Guided **3** | There are various ways materials can be transported across the cell membrane, including active transport.

(a) Give **four** other ways materials can be transported across the cell membrane. 4 marks

1. Osmosis

2. Endocytosis

3. ....

4. ....

(b) Describe the process of active transport. 4 marks

> If you are asked to **describe** something, you need to accurately recall some facts, events or processes. You could write about concentration gradients, energy input and direction of movement.

Active transport requires .... to move materials against a

.... from a region of .... concentration across

a ....

> **Links** You can revise transport across the membrane on pages 50–51 of the Revision Guide.

Guided ❯ 4 | Pangolins are a type of mammal native to Africa and India. A pangolin is shown in the photo below.

(a) Describe **three** features of pangolins which support their classification as mammals. | 3 marks

Think about the characteristics of mammals. Then think about which of these characteristics can be applied to pangolins.

Pangolins give birth to live young. They also ....

....

and ....

....

(b) There are eight species of pangolin. Complete the table to show the levels of classification and the complete taxonomy for pangolins. | 4 marks

Scientific taxonomies are used to classify all animals. For example, a dog is in the kingdom Animalia.

Kingdom	
Phylum	
Class	Mammalia
	Pholidota
Family	Manidae
	Manis
Species	*temminckii*

Pangolins are insectivores that locate their food using a highly developed sense of smell.

(c) Give the name of the type of stimuli this sense relies on. | 1 mark

An **insectivore** is an animal that feeds on insects, worms, and other invertebrates.

.... in the air.

🔗 **Links** | See pages 104–106 of the Revision Guide for more information about the classification of living organisms.

Guided   5   Elephants have a double circulatory system. In this system, blood pumps through the heart twice during each trip around the body.

(a) Explain the advantages of this type of circulatory system.   2 marks

Advantages of a double circulatory system are that there is more .... to the

tissues due to higher .... It also keeps .... separate.

The structure of a mammalian heart is shown below.

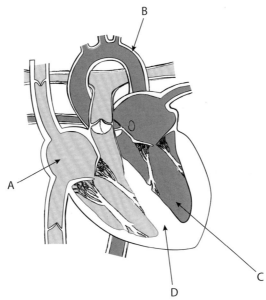

(b) Give the names of the structures labelled A, B, C and D in the diagram.   4 marks

A ....

B ....

C ....

D ....

Possible answers include: aorta, right ventricle, left ventricle, septum, right atrium, left atrium.

(c) Explain how the heartbeat is regulated.   8 marks

It might be useful to start your explanation with the beginning of a heartbeat. Try to include the following structures: sinoatrial node, atrioventricular node, stretch receptors, bundle of His and Purkinje fibres.

Contraction begins at .... , which generates an ....

that spreads through the right .... then the ....

This forces the atria to .... and blood from the atria is forced into the

.... The impulse reaches the .... then travels through

the .... which consists of .... It then goes around the

base of the .... where it causes the ....

(d) State **two** things which can cause changes in heart rate.

2 marks

1. Decrease in blood oxygen levels.

2. ....

(e) Heart murmurs can occur in many species.

Describe **one** cause and **two** symptoms of a heart murmur.

3 marks

Cause: ....

Symptom: coughing

Symptom: ....

> **Links** You can find more information about the cardiac cycle on pages 79–80 of the Revision Guide.

> **Guided** **6** Regulation of body temperature is essential for many processes in the body.

> In biology, regulation is the adaptation of an organism to changed conditions.

(a) Give the normal range of body temperature in mammals.

1 mark

.... °C.

(b) Define the meaning of the term 'endotherm' in animals.

1 mark

The animal is able to maintain ....

....

(c) Explain the process of thermoregulation.

8 marks

> You could make a few notes to help you structure your answer before completing the question. The answer below describes how receptors work to increase body temperature.

Receptors in the .... constantly monitor the .... body

temperature. When they detect a decrease in body temperature, they ....

increase the body temperature such as by ...., ... or shivering.

When the receptors detect that the body temperature has .... to within

..............................., they instruct the response mechanisms to ....,

via a .... loop.

> See pages 101–102 of the Revision Guide for more information about the thermoregulatory system.

> **Guided** 7 In animals, the digestive and excretory systems work together to take in nutrients and remove waste.

(a) Mammals are capable of mechanical and chemical digestion.

Describe the two types of digestion and give an example for each. | 4 marks |

Mechanical digestion is ....

An example of this is ....

Chemical digestion is ....

An example of this is ....

(b) Give the term which describes how food is moved through the digestive tract. | 1 mark |

....

(c) Animals' digestive systems can show anatomical adaptations.

Describe **two** adaptations seen in ruminant digestive systems. | 2 marks |

> Anatomical adaptations are physical features such as an animal's shape or whether the animal has fur.

In a ruminant, the stomach has four chambers. These are the ....

Also in a ruminant, the cecum is ....

(d) State the role of microbes in ruminant digestion. | 2 marks |

Microbes help to digest .... and are a source of ....

> **Guided** 8 DNA instructs how organisms develop and grow by controlling the proteins a cell produces. During protein production, DNA is read in codons.

(a) Identify the complementary base pair for the following bases in DNA. | 2 marks |

| **Thymine** | .... |
| **Cytosine** | .... |

> 🔗 **Links** You can find more information about analysing DNA on page 49 of the Revision Guide.

> Osteogenesis imperfecta is the result of a mutation in the genetic sequence.

(b) Describe **two** symptoms of this disorder. | 2 marks |

> Osteogenesis imperfecta is a disease that causes weak bones that break easily. It is known as 'brittle bone disease'. Sometimes the bones break for no known reason.

....

....

....

....

> **⟨ Links ⟩** You can find more information about genetic disorders on page 49 of the Revision Guide.

 9 Discuss the role of the kidneys in removing waste products from the blood. **8 marks**

> You could write about filtration, concentration gradients, the loop of Henle and molecules that move out of capillaries.

Blood enters the ....under high pressure. This forces small molecules such

as ...., ..., ... and .... out of the capillary and into

the .... Large molecules such as .... remain in the blood.

In the proximal .... glucose, ... and some ions are ....

back into the blood, then in the .... water is absorbed through

.... In the ...., the balance of ions is finely adjusted. Molecules

which are not reabsorbed travel to the ....

> **⟨ Links ⟩** See pages 66–67 of the Revision Guide for more information about the digestive system, and pages 97–100 of the Revision Guide for more information about the excretory system.

END OF REVISION TEST

TOTAL FOR REVISION TASK = 80 MARKS

Revision test 2

This revision test has less support than the first test to allow you to practice the skills and knowledge you have developed.

Answer ALL questions. Write your answers in the spaces provided.

1 The skeletons of animals have evolved over time to provide a range of functions. For example, birds have fewer bones than mammals or reptiles. This makes them lighter for flight.

(a) The diagam below shows the skeleton of a bird. Give the names of structures A, B and C.   3 marks

You might find it helpful to refer to the diagram of a four-legged mammal on page 59 of the Revision Guide. Your answers could include the following: tibia, mandible, ulna, femur, skull.

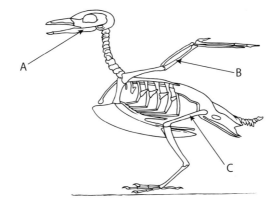

A ....

B ....

C ....

(b) State **four** functions of the skeletons of animals.   4 marks

You should refer to what is produced in bones and what is stored in bones. You should also include the protection that bones provide and the way they help with movement.

....

....

....

....

....

....

....

(c) Explain **two** skeletal adaptations found in birds to allow for flight.

> If you are asked to **explain** something, you need to make it clear, or state the reasons why it happens. You should not just give a list of reasons.

....

....

....

....

....

....

....

....

Links See pages 59–60 of the Revision Guide for more information about the functions of the skeleton.

2 The vertebral column in animals is separated into five sections.

Three of the sections are given below. State the names of the remaining **two** sections.   2 marks

1. Thoracic vertebrae

2. Lumbar vertebrae

3. Sacral vertebrae

4. ....

5. ....

Links You can revise the structure and function of bones on page 60 of the Revision Guide.

3 Owls are predators with forward-facing eyes.

Compare the advantages and disadvantages of forward- and side-facing eyes.   6 marks

....

....

....

....

....

....

....

....

....

....

....

....

> In your answer, you should refer to depth perception, peripheral vision and detecting movement with both forward-facing and side-facing eyes.

> **Links** Eye adaptations are explained on page 77 of the Revision Guide.

4 In order to maintain and promote their health, animals need a balanced diet containing nutrients. Different nutrients have different roles in an animal's body.

(a) Explain the roles of the following nutrients.　　　　　　　　　　　　　　　　`3 marks`

> A nutrient is a substance that provides the nourishment that is essential for life and for growth.

(i) Protein:...

....

(ii) Lipids:..

....

(iii) Carbohydrates:...

....

(b) The majority of nutrients are absorbed in the intestines.
Explain the role of intestinal villi in nutrient uptake.　　　　　　　　　　　`6 marks`

> The inside wall of the small intestine is lined with tiny villi. These stick out and give a large surface area. They also contain blood capillaries to carry away the absorbed food molecules.

....

....

....

....

....

....

....

....

....

....

....

....

....

(c) Cattle are susceptible to ruminant bloat.

State the names of both types of ruminant bloat and the causes of each type. 4 marks

....

....

....

....

....

....

....

> If you are asked to **state** something, you need to accurately recall some facts, events or processes.

> **Links** See pages 66–67 of the Revision Guide for more information about the digestive system and essential nutrients.

5 All animals have **binocular vision**, meaning that they see with two eyes.

The diagram below shows the structure of the eye.

Give the names of the structures labelled A, B, C, D, E and F in the diagram. 6 marks

> Your answers should include: lens, pupil, sclera, cornea, choroid, iris.

A ....

B ....

C ....

D ....

E ....

F ....

6 All animal cells are eukaryotic.

(a) Complete the table to give the functions of each part of a eukaryotic cell. `6 marks`

Eukaryotes are organisms whose cells contain a nucleus surrounded by a membrane. The cells of eukaryotes also contain endoplasmic reticulum as well as mitochondria, Golgi bodies and lysosomes.

Part of cell	Function
Nucleolus	
	Synthesise proteins.
Golgi apparatus	
Mitochondria	
	Regulate what enters and leaves the cell. This also allows the cell to communicate with other cells.
Cytoskeleton	

(b) In cells, there can be two types of endoplasmic reticulum.

Give their names and compare their differences in function. `4 marks`

....

....

....

....

....

....

....

....

Links See pages 46–47 of the Revision Guide for more about the structure of cells.

7 | A scientist is analysing a tissue sample using an electron microscope with magnification of 10 000. The magnified sample shows a cell measuring 7 mm in length.

(a) Calculate the actual size of the cell. `2 marks`

To calculate the actual size of something viewed with a microscope, you need to use the formula:
$$\text{Actual size} = \frac{\text{measured size}}{\text{magnification}}$$

Actual size = ...

Links See page 48 of the Revision Guide for information about calculations when using a microscope.

(b) The cells being observed are from a sample of pseudostratified tissue.

Describe **two** key features of this type of tissue. `2 marks`

Pseudostratified means that the tissue looks as though it is in layers, but is actually a single layer.

....

....

....

....

(c) Compare the differences between simple columnar and stratified squamous epithelial tissue. `2 marks`

In your answer, you should refer to the number of layers and the shape of the cells in each type of tissue.

....

....

....

....

(d) Organs are formed from a range of cells and tissues. Define the term 'tissue'. `2 marks`

....

....

....

....

Links See pages 52–56 of the Revision Guide for more about the structure of animal tissues.

8 | Neurological examination is used by vets to aid in the diagnosis of neurological disease. These tests may include assessing an animal's reflexes, which are non-voluntary responses.

The diagram below shows a non-voluntary reaction.

4 marks

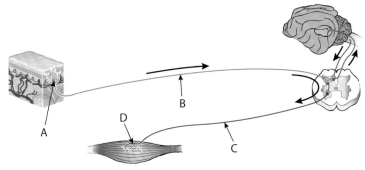

(a) Give the names of the structures involved in the reaction pathway.

A ....

B ....

C ....

D ....

(b) Describe the stages in a non-voluntary reaction.

4 marks

You should begin your answer with the stimulus and end it with the response.

....

....

....

....

....

....

....

....

(c) Describe the role of calcium in the nervous system for propagating action potentials. 2 marks

Include in your answer where the calcium is released from, what it travels across and what it initiates.

....

....

....

....

(d) Explain what is meant by the term 'saltatory conduction'.

2 marks

....

....

....

....

Links See page 72 of the Revision Guide for more about reflexes and responses.

9 Modern technology allows us to use biochemical analysis to explore how animals are related.

Biochemical analysis is used to analyse the substances found in living organisms and the chemical reactions that take place in life processes.

(a) Give **two** techniques which can be used to do this.

2 marks

....

....

....

....

(b) The phylogenetic tree for the toothed whales (Odontoceti) is shown below.

Define the purpose of phylogenetic trees.

1 mark

....

....

(c) *Monodon monoceros* is the scientific name for narwhals.

Give the **two** levels of taxonomy represented by the scientific name.

1 mark

> Scientific taxonomies are used to classify animals to species level.

....

....

(d) Discuss how natural selection and variation have led to speciation in Odontoceti.

8 marks

> In your answer you should refer to variation. You should discuss whether the variation is advantageous, disadvantageous or neutral. Include the effects of advantageous variation on reproduction. You should finish your answer with the effects of increasing genetic variation on reproduction.

....

....

....

....

....

....

....

....

....

....

....

....

....

....

Links You can find out more about taxonomy on pages 104–105 of the Revision Guide.

END OF REVISION TEST

TOTAL FOR REVISION TEST = 80 MARKS

Unit 3: Animal Welfare and Ethics

Your set task

Unit 3 will be assessed through a task, which will be set by Pearson. You will need to use your understanding of animal welfare and ethics, along with your own skills in carrying out research and in assessing information provided to you. After you have carried out this research, you will use your knowledge and understanding to answer questions based on information and scenarios presented to you.

Your Revision Workbook

> This Workbook is designed to **revise skills** that might be needed in your assessed task. The content, outcomes, questions and answers are provided to help you to revise content and ways of applying your skills. Ask your tutor or check the Pearson website for the most up-to-date **Sample Assessment Material** and **Mark Scheme** to get an indication of the structure of your assessed task and what this requires of you. Notice the example given in relation to the task given, the amount of time given for research and for the set task, as well as whether or not you may bring notes into the assessment. The details of the actual assessed task may change so always make sure you are up to date.

This Workbook contains revision tasks to help you revise the skills that might be needed in your assessed task. In Unit 3, the revision tasks are divided into two sections.

1 Research

In this Workbook you will use your skills to:
- plan your time and how you will tackle your research (pages 55 and 85)
- read and make notes on a provided scenario (pages 54 and 85)
- carry out your own independent secondary research related to the scenario provided (pages 56–66 and 86–89)
- assess the stimulus material provided to identify relevant information and any gaps in what you need to know (pages 67–71 and 90–94).

2 Questions

Your response to the questions will help you to revise:
- writing an **appraisal report** (page 72–76 and 95–97)
- assessing **how comprehensive** this appraisal report can be, given the information provided and assessing what **further information** is needed (pages 77–78 and 98–100)
- creating an **action plan** (pages 79–80 and 101–103)
- considering **ethical issues** involved in a given scenario (pages 81–84 and 104–106).

> To help you revise skills that you might need in your Unit 3 set task, this Workbook contains two revision tasks starting on pages 54 and 85.
>
> See the introduction on page iii for more information on the features included to help you revise.

Revision task 1

To answer the revision activities, you will need to carefully read through the task brief, carry out your initial research into the issues around the subject and thoroughly read through the stimulus materials provided.

In your actual assessment:
- The task brief and stimulus materials will be new each year, and the secondary research sources you will need to find to relate to it will change.
- You may not be allowed to use your preparatory notes, or there may be restrictions on the length and type of preparatory notes that are allowed. Check with your tutor or look at the latest Sample Assessment Material on the Pearson website for details.

You need to make sure you use your research time wisely, by reading the scenario carefully, planning how to use your time, and making useful notes that will be helpful in answering the questions in your assessed task.

Plan your research based on this and the time you have available to you, taking into account your own understanding of the Unit 3 content.

Below you will find an example task brief and information to try.

Task brief

You are required to carry out research into the scenario provided in the task information below. You should consider the following areas in relation to the scenario:
- legislation and regulations relating to the animal species
- policies and practices relating to the setting and linkages to the welfare requirements of that species
- ethical issues relating to ownership of the species.

Task information

Superpets is a large pet store retailer that wants to open a new pet superstore in an out-of-town retail outlet. They have applied to the local council for a licence under the Pet Animals Act 1951.

You work for the council and have been asked to carry out an appraisal with recommendations for Superpets.

Over the next pages, you will find guidance and support on how to respond to this task information, including how to plan your time, carry out your own preparatory research and make notes. You will need to read the information supplied to you carefully. You should start to think about the legislation mentioned within the task information and make sure you are familiar with the requirements of obtaining a licence.

 Links See page 140 of the Revision Guide for information surrounding the Pet Animals Act (1951).

Plan your research

You may have a limited time to carry out your research. It is really important that you use your time wisely. By spending 10 minutes planning at the start, you will ensure that you cover all the key points that you need to research and leave yourself enough time to make a good set of notes.

Use the table below to create your own plan for researching into this revision task, to ensure you are clear on the areas you need to cover. You might choose a different way of planning your time, but this example should help to get you started.

You should check with your tutor or on the Pearson website for the specification and Sample Assessment Material for guidance on how long you will have to prepare.

Stage	Done
Read the task information and identify which areas need further research.	☐
Research legislation and regulations relating to animal species likely to be kept in a pet shop.	☐
Research policies and practices relating to pet shops, covering how this relates to welfare requirements of pet animal species.	☐
Explore ethical issues to consider in relation to pet shops.	☐
Organise my notes.	☐

Use this space to add in any other areas you feel would be useful to research.

....
....
....
....
....
....
....
....
....
....
....
....
....
....
....
....

Legislation

Think about the main legislation that applies to a pet shop.

You should make notes on both the Pet Animals Act (1951) and the Animal Welfare Act (2006). You can access legislative requirements from legislation.gov.uk, but be sure to summarise key points of the legislation so your notes are clear and concise.

When making notes consider specific examples, for instance, rather than just writing 'age of selling mammals', you will better demonstrate your understanding by being more specific and state the age at which they can be sold.

The example below shows one way of summarising the key points of the Pet Animals Act (1951).

Pet Animals Act (1951)

Purpose of the legislation

The purpose is to consider the welfare of animals kept in pet shops with respect to their needs, whether they are kept in short- or long-term accommodation.

Parties involved

Local authorities and veterinary surgeons/practitioners are involved.

Conditions

Specific conditions must be met before a licence can be granted from the local authority, and to ensure adherence once a licence has been granted. Inspections can be carried out at any time without warning. Conditions include:

- Animals will be kept in suitable accommodation at all times, for example:
  - **Size** – minimum enclosure size requirements for species and number of animals to be housed are provided by welfare organisations.
  - **Cleanliness** – animals should be cleaned frequently, e.g. spot-cleaned daily, disinfected weekly.
  - **Ventilation** – e.g. mice will require good ventilation and can often have wire mesh lids on their enclosures.
  - **Temperature** – e.g. reptiles and amphibians will require a warmer, more humid environment, for example bearded dragons should have gradient temperatures at either end of their enclosure.
  - **Lighting** – animals should be subjected to 'normal' light and dark cycles.
- Animals will be given suitable food and drink for their species-specific requirements.
- Animals will be visited at suitable intervals, e.g. animals with young may need to be checked three or four times a day, whereas a general morning and night check may be sufficient for other animals.
- Mammals must not be sold at too early an age, generally, at eight weeks of age mammals are fully weaned and can be taken away from their mother.
- Disease precautions will be taken as a preventative measure, e.g. hand washing facilities, PPE available, disinfectants used regularly.
- Fire and other emergency procedures/steps are in place as a preventative measure, e.g. fire blankets and extinguishers in appropriate places, first aid kit and first aiders on site.

 There is more support on legislation on pages 137–145 of the Revision Guide.

Five animal needs

 Make some notes on the Animal Welfare Act 2006 by completing the student notes in the table below. Ensure you provide specific examples as detailed on the previous page.

Animal need	Interpretation	Species-specific example
Need for a suitable environment	All animals kept in a pet store should have an environment similar to what they would have in the wild.	Zebra finches should be kept in a suitable .... which includes perches, enough ...., ventilation and is secure.
Need for a suitable	All animals kept in a pet store should have the correct diet – this includes both .... provision, supplementation and ...., supplied at appropriate intervals.	Bearded dragons should be supplied with .... and vegetables, as well as live feed (............... and locusts, for example). They should be given appropriate supplements, including vitamin D3 and ....
Need to be able to exhibit normal .... patterns	All animals kept in a pet store should have facilities to encourage .... behaviour. This could be in the form of enrichment and .... design.	Rodent species could be supplied with nesting material such as ...., ... or hay. They could also be given items to gnaw on such as ...., ... apparatus would also be appropriate such as ladders, swings and ....
Need to be housed with, or apart from, other	All animals kept in a pet store should have a similar social structure to what they would experience in the wild. This includes whether they are .... (live alone) or .... (group living) species.	Rodents can be either solitary and group living. Syrian hamster: .... animal that should be housed .... as .... Rats: ....
Need to be protected from pain, suffering, injury and disease		Rabbits should be .... at appropriate ages, and be provided with regular wormers and .... treatments. .... should remain safe and secure at all times, so that public .... If rabbits fight they should be .... where appropriate.

Welfare considerations

Now you should explore and make notes on aspects of animal welfare relating to pet shops. Complete the sample notes before regarding general aspects of suitable environments for animals being housed in a pet shop.

The correct environment for exotic species

It can be hard to replicate natural environments, particularly size – many captive animals need much more space than we can allow.

Key aspects of suitable environment

- **Size/space** – all dimensions need to be considered. Animals will use .... as well

  as .... and .... Animals may climb, swing, fly, swim or travel long

  distances which cannot always be provided in captivity.

- **Enrichment** – can natural environments be recreated? Generally, they can be hard to create, and in

  captivity we often use artificial structures and .... e.g. plastic hides and treat balls.

  Hygiene issues accompany natural enrichment like trees, logs, pools and rocks when it comes to

  disease control (they are harder to .... and remove, etc.).

- **Temperature and ventilation** – some species require environments that may be harder to recreate,

  e.g. .... It can be hard to provide wild environments in

  countries that do not experience similar weather, e.g. keeping Australia's native species in the UK

  requires certain equipment (bulbs, heat mats, etc.).

- **Light/dark cycles** – it is natural for animals to have light and dark cycles. Their behaviour and

  feeding patterns may rely on this. Artificial lights in some enclosures are not always ideal,

  particularly if bulbs do not emit ....

- **Using equipment and barriers** – some can be unsuitable for species, e.g. wooden barriers may not

  be ideal for animals that may .... Similarly, there are issues relating to using some

  types of equipment such as .... Using heat mats and bulbs for reptiles can be

  detrimental to health because ....

Complete the notes in the table below regarding the potential impact of environment on the behaviour of animals.

<u>Behaviour of animals in captivity</u>

It can be hard to replicate natural environments which may encourage natural behaviours. In many cases the captive environment can create stereotypical behaviours. Stereotypical behaviours are considered abnormal behaviours that are not seen in these species in the wild, see table below.

Examples of stereotypical behaviour	Example species	Causes of stereotypical behaviour
Bar biting – animals will constantly gnaw or chew at the bars of their enclosure.	Pigs	It is usually caused by an animal's environment. Here are some examples of where issues can arise: **Lack of size and space** – some animals travel miles each day in a container, or need to frequently have new areas to explore.
.... – birds can self-harm by using their beak to painfully remove feathers.	Birds, particularly parrot species such as African Grey Parrots	**Little** .... – lack of stimulation is provided in general, and new stimulation is not given regularly.
Weaving and head bobbing – animals will repeatedly move their heads from side to side (weaving) or up and down (head bobbing).	....	**Interactions** – many species need to socialise and smaller environments do not allow for this.
.... – animal will constantly lick and nibble their fur or skin, causing irritation, redness, and sometimes broken skin.	Dogs	**Natural** .... – artificial environments are often provided. **Feeding** – food is given to the animals rather than them .... or hunting it as they would naturally.

You should be able to find out other relevant information to include in your notes on behaviour and welfare You can record these in the space below.

....
....
....
....
....
....
....
....
....
....
....

Welfare requirements

You should make notes on how a pet store can accommodate specific animals. Consider species that you would commonly find within a pet store, particularly from different groups, for example mammals, birds and reptiles.

You could consider these species in relation to diets, enrichment types, aspects of accommodation and so on. Welfare organisations usually have this information available so check out these sources as well as the relevant legislative requirements such as those found at legislation.gov.uk.

Using the notes below as a guide, make notes for each of the following pet species:

- bearded dragons

- guinea pigs

Complete the example notes that are provided.

How you make the notes is up to you – different styles suit different people and the type of information that is being recorded. For instance, you could write the notes out in sentences or you might prefer to list some bullet points, create a table or make a mind map.

<u>Bearded dragons</u>

<u>Diet</u>

Firstly, research what components make up a bearded dragon's diet. You should be considering food types, water and supplements.

Live feed: depends on size and age of the bearded dragon, e.g. adults can eat mealworms, waxworms, locusts and crickets

Fruit and vegetables: e.g. carrots, cabbage, parsnips and kale, apples, strawberries, pears and melon

Diet

Calcium and vitamin D3: important for the lizard's bone strength and development. They can easily develop metabolic bone disease if not provided with the correct vitamins and minerals.

Water: ....

....

....

<u>Environment</u>

Now consider how it is possible to replicate their natural environment. You should think about visual appearance, as well as external factors relating to normal functions, such as temperature.

External factors:

- Temperature is important for bearded dragons as they come from a hot climate.

- An area should be provided to obtain maximum temperature with a gradient that allows them to cool down if they need to.

- The hottest temperature is usually around .... degrees Celsius, where the cooler end is around

  .... degrees Celsius (usually a range to account for different ages).

- Not only does the bearded dragon require a light for heat, but also to absorb

  .... as it is likely to have little access to the Sun, unlike in the wild.

- Ventilation is important to ensure a flow of fresh air.

 There is more support on how to ensure high levels of animal welfare on page 114 of the Revision Guide, including accommodation, feeding and enrichment.

Enrichment:

Creating an environment where they have similar substrate to their wild environment is beneficial.

Sand, or similar material, is good for burrowing and performing natural behaviours, but need to avoid

ingesting (leading to ....).

Reptile carpets also give the appearance of a natural environment, e.g. grassy or desert habitats.

Objects that would be found in the wild, such as ...., logs and pebbles, are good for

.... and should be placed in the correct areas of the accommodation.

Food is also a good method of enrichment, as .... can be provided to the bearded

dragons so that they can chase and catch their prey.

> Finally, consider the accommodation materials suitable for a bearded dragon. You could look at different accommodation materials and evaluate their suitability.

Accommodation materials

Material	Advantages	Disadvantages
Glass	Easy to clean Can visually check lizard without too much disturbance Holds heat well	Heavy .... Need to take care that lizard isn't burnt on hot glass
Plastic	Light and easy to	Usually smaller accommodation, so more suited to younger bearded dragons such as those only a few months old Does not hold .... as well as glass Not compatible with some heat sources
Wood	Aesthetically pleasing Useful when housing several types of animals (solid walls so animals cannot see each other) Most heat sources can be used within	Can be heavy Care must be taken with heat and wood but there are options for installing heat lamps safely.

> Now make your own notes on some other species.

Guinea pigs

Diet

> What important components make up a guinea pig's diet?

....

....

....

....

....

Environment

How can you replicate their natural environment?

....

....

....

....

....

....

....

Accommodation materials

What accommodation materials are suited to a guinea pig?

....

....

....

....

....

....

....

....

....

....

....

....

....

....

....

....

There are other pet species you could research including birds, rabbits, other small mammals and exotics. Make a list of other species you could research. If you have time, you could use the topics on the previous pages as a guide to carrying out your own research.

....

....

....

....

....

....

....

....

....

....

....

....

....

....

....

....

....

....

General practices

Consider general housekeeping and safety routines in a pet store. These will usually follow guidelines on frequency of cleaning and maintaining accommodation, as well as disinfecting the shop and completing stock takes (both of animals and non-livestock items). Complete the example notes below on important general practices in a pet shop.

Safety precautions can be noted here, such as fire policy, checks on security and animal accommodation, and animal health routines that will contribute to disease prevention.

 Links You can revise general housekeeping and safety precautions on page 140 of the Revision Guide.

Purpose and frequency of security checking

- General checking of animal accommodation would fall within routine daily checks, probably at the beginning and end of the day.
- Ensure all animals are still in their accommodation, are safe and contained within their area, e.g. to prevent disease spreading, fighting and unplanned breeding.

- Security checks should be made every evening when the shop shuts to ensure the premises are secured overnight.

> There will always be changes to routines, for example due to number of animals in enclosure, illness or the animals' life stages

Species	Cleaning routine	Accommodation checks
Rat	**Spot clean** – daily (except on days where full clean/disinfect may be completed) to remove old pellets, food and waste material such as soiled shavings. **Full clean** – once per week to remove all shavings, nesting material and enrichment and replace. **Disinfect** – once per week (same as full clean but disinfect before replacing clean shavings and enrichment).	• Check locks/latch morning and evening. • Check safety of enrichment, particularly where plastic can be gnawed. • Check condition of bars, to ensure they are not sharp and that animals cannot escape.
Corn snake	Spot clean – .... (except ....) to remove .... such as soiled lining paper or substrate. Full clean – .... to remove and replace all substrate, e.g. paper. Disinfect – .... (same as full clean, but disinfect before replacing clean paper and enrichment).	• Check locks/latch .... • Check condition of .... • Check condition of vivarium to ensure it is safe and .... • Check .... and heat source (not exposed or broken).
Budgie	Spot clean – .... (except ....) to remove .... Full clean – .... Disinfect – .... (same as full clean, but ....).	• Check locks/latch in the morning and evening. • Check safety of perches and other enrichment devices, as well as nest boxes. • Check condition of bars, to ensure they are not sharp and that animals cannot escape.
Bearded dragon	Spot clean – .... Full clean – .... Disinfect –	• .... • .... • Check condition of vivarium to ensure .... • Check temperature and ....

Ethics

Research the ethical issues that might arise from owning a pet store. Also think about the issues of keeping exotic species and how they may be sourced. Make notes based on this research. You could research and answer questions like:

Who are the stakeholders when considering opening up a pet store and how may this influence an ethical matrix?

What may the different ethical theories include?

Should we **breed** animals for the purpose of keeping them as pets?

The example below shows one way of summarising the key points when considering the ethics of keeping exotic animals in captivity. Complete the sections where information is missing.

If you search for 'pets and ethics' online, you should find some reputable websites that cover these issues. Remember to research the problems that arise when keeping pets in a captive and home environment. You may want to think about animal welfare, and how mimicking their natural environment and freedom may benefit them.

The Journal of Animal Ethics contains up-to-date information about animals and morality, as well as expert opinions, particularly towards current affairs.

Remember there are different stakeholders to consider when making decisions about keeping pets, as well as different ethical principles.

<u>Who are the stakeholders when considering opening up a pet store and how may this influence an</u>
<u>ethical matrix?</u>

Stakeholders could include:

- animals
- pet owners/customers
- consumers
  - ◦ pet store owner
  - ◦ breeders
  - ◦ veterinary staff.

You could use an ethical matrix such as the one given below. Complete the missing entries.

	Health and welfare	Freedom and choice	Fairness
Animals	Animal welfare and conservation		Intrinsic value of animals
Pet owners/customers		Freedom of action	Compliance with legislation
Consumers	Good income and working conditions	Options based on information supplied	

....

....

....

....

....

....

<u>What may the different ethical theories include?</u>

Some examples of ethical theories include duty ethics (deontology) where keeping pets is important for humans, particularly those species that a strong bond can be formed with, for example, cats, rabbits (relational importance). But on the other hand, considering animal rights may infer that animals should not be kept as pets (although this would be dependent on how well the animals are kept – perhaps heavily related to their welfare).

> Think about environmental ethics and make some notes on how this can apply to a pet store setting. When considering your answers, you need to think about all opinions linked to the scenario, ensuring you explore several viewpoints.

....

....

....

....

....

....

....

....

....

....

....

....

 Links Visit page 132 of the Revision Guide to look at sentience-centre, human-centred and environment centred ethics.

✎ Organise your notes

You may be allowed to take some of your preparatory notes into your supervised assessment time. If so, there may be restrictions on the length and type of notes that are allowed. Check with your tutor or look at the latest Sample Assessment Material on the Pearson website for more information.

To answer the revision activities that follow on pages 72–84, as well as your notes from the previous pages, you will also need to refer to the stimulus material provided below. You should carefully read any of the stimulus materials you are given in order to understand what information these contain.

Stimulus material

The stimulus material contains extra information that you will need to use to answer the activities in the revision task. Read through the stimulus material and make notes on the strengths and weaknesses of the materials given, how well they meet legal requirements and any ways you can see they could be improved.

The following stimulus material has been collected for you:
- Superpets staff procedures when selling animals
- Superpets fire precautions
- Superpets new store design – floor plan
- Superpets accommodation requirements
- Superpets animal health.

Superpets staff procedures when selling animals

- No animal will be sold to any person under the age of 16 without a parent or legal guardian present or sufficient evidence of consent.
- Animals can be sold to a person over 12 but under 16 if a parent or legal guardian is present.
- Animals will not be sold to children under 12, even with legal consent.
- Sufficient consent may be in the form of a letter or email – however, the manager must be happy that the evidence supplied is genuine.
- Checks to be made that adequate care and attention will be provided to the animal, for example via a questionnaire or oral questioning.
- Animals will be health checked before putting them into temporary accommodation for transporting to the new owner's home. Staff must be happy the animal is in good health before completing the sale.
- A new owner form must be completed then added to the database after sale.
- Information leaflets should be supplied to the new owner relating to the species that has been purchased.
- Remind customers of the one week returns policy.

NB: Staff procedures when selling animals are not listed in a specific order of events.

Superpets provides a checklist for staff to use when selling live animals. Use the space below to make notes on areas such as:
- How often and how thoroughly are the animals are all checked?
- How much information are customers given on their chosen animal, how to transport and care for it?
- What checks are made on customer suitability?
- Do the procedures conform to legislation?

....

....

....

....

Superpets fire precautions

This information is displayed on the health and safety notice board found in the staff-only area, and is also detailed in the staff handbook.

- If you notice a fire, raise the alarm by pulling the lever on the fire alarm. One is located in the stock room, and another near the customer entrance/exit.

- Direct all customers and staff to the designated evacuation points at the other side of the customer car park.

- Dial 999 if the fire is considered serious.

- Fire extinguishers and fire blankets are provided in designated areas of the store. You should only use a fire extinguisher or blanket if you have completed fire safety training.

- People first: attempt to evacuate all customers and staff before considering evacuating animals.

- Where possible, animals should be safely evacuated to the designated emergency shelter as quickly as possible.

- Only attempt to put out a fire or rescue animals if it is safe to do so.

- Do not put yourself or others in danger.

NB: Fire precautions are not listed in a specific order of events.

Superpets provides information about fire precautions on site. Make some notes, considering questions such as:
- Is there enough information on what to do in a fire for staff, customers and animals?
- Is all relevant equipment provided?
- Does the document conform to relevant legislation?
- Is any relevant information about training and fire officers provided?
- Are evacuation procedures for animals clear and comprehensive?

Think about this document when considering the safety of the customers, staff and animals at Superpets. Have all aspects been taken into account?

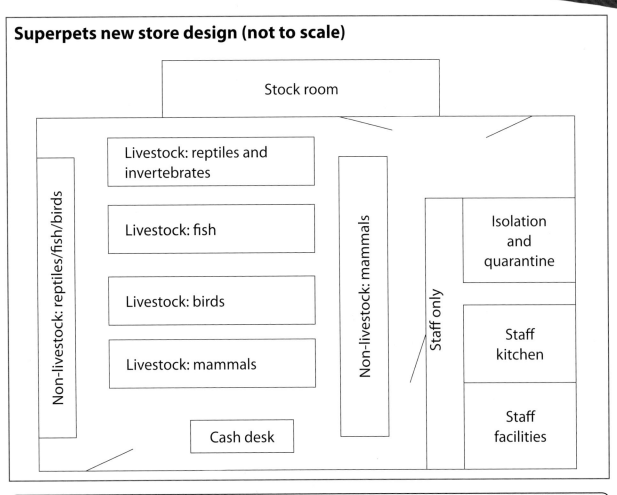

Superpets new store design (not to scale)

The store design is important as it can show where both livestock and non-livestock items are kept in the store. Make your own notes, thinking about the following questions:
- Is the plan detailed enough?
- Is it clear from the information supplied whether all legislation is being followed?
- What else would you expect to see in a plan like this?

....
....
....
....
....
....
....
....
....
....
....
....
....

Superpets animal accommodation requirements

The animals' environment must be correct at all times. The accommodation must also be kept in a good state of repair. This will include the following considerations:

- temperature
- ventilation
- lighting
- cleanliness
- size
- draughts
- location of livestock.

Other considerations to be accounted for:

- Hygiene and cleanliness must be maintained regularly.
- Stacked accommodation must retain materials – no food or faecal matter can easily escape and enter accommodation below.
- Make species considerations with regards to predator and prey relations.
- Considerations need to be made for those animals housed inside or outside: appropriate amendments for species and acclimatisation.
- Construction materials must be suitable for species and maintenance by staff.
- Security provision should be made on all enclosures regardless of species.
- All accommodation types must be easily accessed by staff, for example consider height and weight of accommodation if it requires moving for access.
- Suitable enrichment types must be provided to animals and can easily be maintained within the accommodation types, for example enrichment is easy to remove and clean as above.

Superpets provides an information list for staff to consider when housing live animals.

Think about this document when considering animal welfare. Have all aspects been taken into account?

Consider the following points and make notes below:
- Is the information supplied sufficient for staff to know how to care for animals?
- Does it conform to relevant legislation?
- Have all aspects of accommodation been considered?

....

....

....

....

....

....

....

....

....

....

....

Superpets animal health policy

All animals on sale should be in good health and free from disease – no animal showing signs of abnormalities or illness should be sold.

The following procedure should be completed by the first member of staff on shift every morning. It should also be completed by the last staff member on shift. These should be completed outside of the customer opening hours.

- Monitor all sale animals for signs of good health, for example expected activity levels; enclosure and animal is clear of discharge and blood.

- Complete record books detailing findings.

- Isolate sick or injured animals away from the customer area and the rest of the animals on sale. Monitor them regularly, ensuring they have access to the correct care and treatment immediately (if required).

- Euthanasia must be completed by a trained professional or the animal taken to a veterinary surgeon.

- Use personal protective equipment (PPE) when completing physical health checks, for example latex or nitrile gloves, face mask, apron.

- Ensure that the correct hygiene and disinfectant procedures are in place to eliminate the risk of spreading disease, for example cleaning surfaces regularly, washing hands.

- Animals vaccinations must be maintained at the correct intervals, for example annually.

- New animals should be quarantined and allowed to acclimatise before being introduced to a new group and put on sale.

- Young mammals should be fully weaned before being separated from their mother, for example at around 8–10 weeks of age.

Superpets provides staff with a procedure for checking the health of livestock. Use the space below to make your own notes, considering questions such as:
- Is the policy clear and complete?
- Is it thorough enough to ensure animal health issues are picked up rapidly?
- Is there enough information given about record keeping?
- Is any relevant legislation followed?

Think about this document when considering animal welfare. Have all aspects been taken into account?

Guided **Writing an appraisal report**

You may be asked to write an appraisal report based on the information supplied in the task brief and the stimulus material. The main skills you need to practise are:
- assessing information in the stimulus materials against legal requirements
- writing a balanced report on what is done well and not so well
- structuring a longer piece of writing well and ensuring it makes a clear argument.

To do this, you need to carefully read all the information provided on pages 67–71 and ensure you understand it. Keep asking questions about the material – does it cover everything? Is there anything unexpected? Where are the obvious gaps?

You can mark it up using your own system – for example, underlining or highlighting important points, or writing a question mark next to content you think needs to be queried. You could also make your own notes from the information, perhaps rearranging it into topics.

The example below shows an example of how you could annotate the materials.

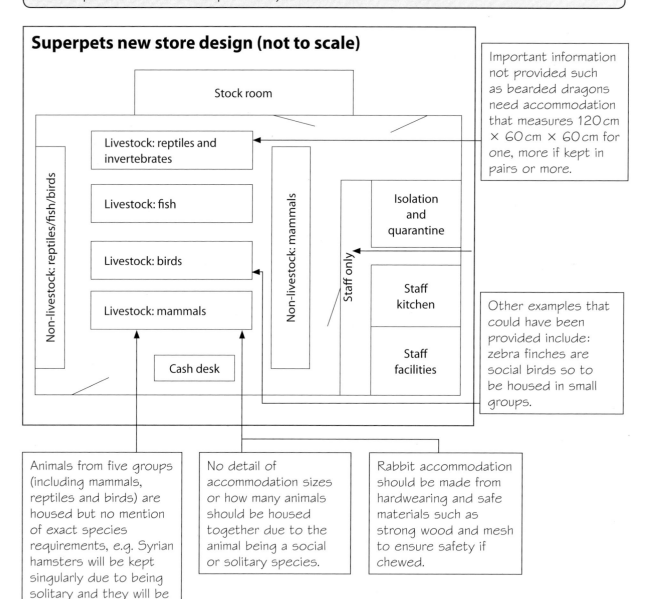

Superpets new store design (not to scale)

Stock room

Livestock: reptiles and invertebrates

Livestock: fish

Livestock: birds

Livestock: mammals

Non-livestock: reptiles/fish/birds

Non-livestock: mammals

Staff only

Isolation and quarantine

Staff kitchen

Staff facilities

Cash desk

Important information not provided such as bearded dragons need accommodation that measures 120 cm × 60 cm × 60 cm for one, more if kept in pairs or more.

Other examples that could have been provided include: zebra finches are social birds so to be housed in small groups.

Animals from five groups (including mammals, reptiles and birds) are housed but no mention of exact species requirements, e.g. Syrian hamsters will be kept singularly due to being solitary and they will be fed once a day.

No detail of accommodation sizes or how many animals should be housed together due to the animal being a social or solitary species.

Rabbit accommodation should be made from hardwearing and safe materials such as strong wood and mesh to ensure safety if chewed.

Write an appraisal report of Superpets' planned new pet store. Using the additional information provided, you should address:

- how Superpets plans to meet its legal requirements for animal welfare when selling and keeping a range of animals
- how Superpets plans to meet the health and welfare needs of the animals in its care
- ethical issues related to Superpets' animal welfare considerations.

> This is a long-answer question, so you should spend some time planning what you might write about.
>
> Use the example plan started for you below to create an outline for your response. Make sure you plan to cover all three bullet points in order, to ensure that your response is well structured.
>
> A good starting point is to consider relevant legislation:
>
> - **Pet Animals Act (1951)** – this is the main focus of obtaining a licence and addressing key areas within a pet store. Think about the factors that would stop a business from getting a licence, for example animal accommodation requirements.
>
> - **Animal Welfare Act (2006)** – the key focus is the welfare of the animals that are to be sold. Is it obvious how their basic needs have or have not been met? Remember the five animal needs.

Legal requirements

- Pet Animals Act (1951) – evidence that it has been adhered to:

  Positives: animals' health checked before sale, mammals weaned before sale, customers must be over 16.

  Negatives: not enough information on accommodation to know whether correct sizes, construction materials etc. supplied.

- Animal Welfare Act (2006) – evidence that it has been adhered to:

  Positives: animals are vaccinated, monitored and checked daily, suitable isolation and quarantine areas provided along with enrichment.

  Negatives: no information on feeding of animals, no mention of access to external environment, but no reference to (e.g.) UV lamps for bearded dragons or procedures to check these are working if supplied.

  Stimulus material to reference: store layout plan, animal health policy, accommodation requirements, procedures when selling animals.

  Conclusion: information basic but the essentials are there.

Health and welfare needs

Consider how the animal's health and welfare has or has not been maintained.

Positives:

- Again animals are health checked before sale, as well as monitored for signs of good health specific to species (activity for example).

  ....

  ....

Negatives:

- Accommodation information does not provide depth (e.g. size).

- ....

Stimulus material to reference: ....

....

<u>Ethical issues related to animal welfare</u>

Look at some of the information supplied by Superpets and provide a balanced overview of the ethical considerations:

- Animals are sentient beings and therefore should be provided with the correct environment and

  conditions – Superpets do a relatively good job at maintaining welfare such as ....

- On the other hand, ...

<u>Conclusion</u>

Cover both plus and minus points, make clear which are the key issues:

- Evidence that legislation has been followed (e.g. ages of customers, ages of animals sold)
- Legislation, welfare, ethics all covered in some respects (e.g. accommodation needs, emergency procedures, reducing ill health)

- However, ...

- Rank the issues discussed in terms of ....

> An example response is below, where the student clearly refers to these Acts and identifies where Superpets has – and then perhaps has not – met its legal requirements.

Superpets has considered several aspects of the Pet Animals Act (1951) by providing a variety of procedures and documentation to its staff members. Firstly, there is clear evidence relating to the sale of the animals, both in terms of the animals' health and age of sale. All animals must be health checked before sale, checked twice a day before being on display to the public, and not sold until

fully weaned for mammals (usually between 8–10 weeks). Superpets also refers to ....

....

....

However, there is little evidence to suggest Superpets will provide suitable accommodation for the

animals. ....

....

....

....

> ✎ Now consider the Animal Welfare Act (2006). Briefly refer to each element to assess whether Superpets has considered all aspects and to what depth. It has been started for you. Continue the answer with reference to the Animal Welfare Act (2006).

In relation to the Animal Welfare Act (2006), there is no mention of animals having access to ....

....

....

....

> As well as referring to the legislation, the student gives specific examples from the stimulus material. This makes the answer more focused and helps to structure it.

....

....

....
....
....
....
....
....
....

> Start by reviewing the stimulus material to see if there is any mention of enrichment being provided and whether it is suitable. Also consider accommodation space in a pet store compared to space in the wild. When you feel you have covered all relevant legal requirements, you can move onto the second bullet point in the question by considering accommodation space and enrichment in relation to ethical issues.
>
> The example answer starts with a general statement and then considers some examples that could be applied to ethical issues.

Overall, the health and welfare needs of the animals have been addressed. However, this is basic and Superpets could address these needs in greater depth. It discusses regularly checking the animals each day and highlights the need for disease prevention. Checking the animals' health regularly will determine their condition and allows staff to implement health care, and the policy for euthanising if necessary. It also highlights the need for staff to wear the correct PPE to reduce the potential spread of infectious diseases. This is also reiterated in the housekeeping and cleanliness of staff, for example disinfecting surfaces regularly as well as hand washing.

> Continue the answer with further references to the ethical issues raised by the stimulus material. You could use the store layout to detail how the needs of the animals have been met in terms of attempting to reduce their stress, and to consider the location of isolation and quarantine facilities.

....
....
....
....
....
....
....
....
....
....
....

Now make sure you draw your answer together with a short conclusion - one has been started for you.

Superpets consider several aspects within their new plans. They provide information that indicates legislation has been considered, including ages of customers purchasing pets, as well as the animals to be sold. Legislation, welfare and ethics are also linked with regards to catering for the animal's accommodation needs, emergency procedures, regular checks and plans to reduce ill health. With all three areas there are factors that have not had sufficient consideration. For example, ...

....

....

....

....

....

....

....

....

....

....

....

....

....

....

....

....

....

....

....

....

....

....

....

Links See page 115 of the Revision Guide for more information about animal welfare in captivity.

Guided ## Assessing the stimulus material

> You may be asked to consider how comprehensive the stimulus material is – do you need more information to be able to write a comprehensive appraisal? If so, what sort of information do you need? Use the activity below to practise this skill.

To what extent does the information in the stimulus material allow for a comprehensive appraisal to be conducted? In your answer you must refer to any additional information you would need in order to complete a comprehensive appraisal report.

> This is a long-answer question so you need to spend some time planning what you might write about. Your response will need to make reference to the stimulus material on pages 67–71.
>
> As for the previous question, you need to develop a logical argument, with a clear and well organised structure. The key is to approach the stimulus material logically, assessing what information has been provided and identifying any gaps. This will help you to stick to the point and ensure your response remains relevant. You will waste your time if you write additional points that do not answer the question.
>
> A good way of ensuring you have covered all the relevant points is to create a table like the one below. This should not form your final answer but can be used to structure your written answer and make sure you don't miss anything.

Documentation	Included – some examples	Missing - some examples
Superpets staff procedures when selling animals	Thorough selling procedure that takes into account legislative requirements	Specific sequence of events Example of forms used to assess whether customers are suitable
Superpets fire precautions	Equipment accounted for	Emergency procedures and responsibilities
Superpets new store design – floor plan	Important aspects considered, for example isolation facilities	Species-specific information including dimensions of the store/accommodation
Accommodation requirements	Basic overview of accommodation requirements	Specific examples including species information
Animal health procedure	Consideration of number of checks to be completed PPE encouraged	Information in relation to time to be spent in isolation/quarantine (as a guide)

> The example extract below builds on some of the information in the table.
>
> Continue the answer by using the stimulus material to consider the following questions:
> - Are the emergency and evacuation procedures clear, including general escape routes?
> - Have different species been placed in a good location for them?
> - How do store procedures meet legislative requirements? Are they realistic?

The accommodation requirements documentation provides a basic overview of considerations for animals housed at Superpets. This includes important factors such as lighting, heating and acclimatisation. It would be helpful for Superpets to provide a document for each of the commonly kept species on the premises, for example rabbits, mice, bearded dragons and corn snakes. These could contain, for example, information about temperature gradients, suitable size of accommodation, whether the species should be housed together, and breeding information to ensure this is accounted for in the animals' accommodation. This would indicate that the pet store management is knowledgeable about species requirements, and can guide staff accordingly.

Creating an action plan

> You may be asked to create an action plan to address any weaknesses you have identified in your appraisal. The action plan needs to give specific actions, reasons for these and timescales. Use the activity below to practise your skills of identifying what needs to be done, suggesting actions and expressing your ideas clearly.

Produce an action plan for Superpets to address the issues identified in your appraisal. Your action plan must make reference to:
- actions required by the Superpets management
- reasons for the actions
- timescales for the actions to be completed.

> This is a long-answer question so you need to spend some time planning what you might write about.
>
> Firstly, remind yourself about the purpose of an action plan. Action plans are a set of detailed instructions, or actions needed to achieve goal(s): their purpose is to provide realistic and achievable goals to an intended audience.
>
> Three key areas are required when creating an action plan:
> - **Actions**: Think about what you highlighted on pages 77 and 78 that is missing or could be improved. Also consider the order of priority in which actions need to be completed to ensure the pet store is ready for inspection.
> - **Why**: Explain why these actions need to be taken. This could be related to a current failure to meet legislative requirements or welfare needs, for example.
> - **Timescale**: Is there an expectation that actions are completed instantly, for example to address welfare issues, or can some be postponed to allow more urgent issues to take precedent? The example below uses the key areas above as headings to organise the answer.

.Action

Provide detailed species-specific accommodation information.

Why?

The current Superpets accommodation requirements document is very basic and does not provide sufficient species-specific information. It is unclear whether legislation is followed or if animal welfare is maintained. For example, the Animal Welfare Act (2006) requires animals to be housed in suitable accommodation, but there is no evidence to suggest the animals at Superpets are suitably accommodated.

Timescale/urgency

The detailed information needs to be provided in the next few weeks before further inspections.

It is not urgent as it may be assumed the accommodation is suitable, but it is not documented within the information supplied.

> 🔗 **Links** You can find more information about action plans in the Revision Guide on page 154.

Continue the action plan for other aspects you may have highlighted as 'missing' when looking through the stimulus material. You could think about the lack of information about emergency procedures, such as who to report to in an emergency.

Remember to structure your action plan to include what the action is, why it is needed and the timescale or urgency of completing the action.

....

....

....

....

....

....

....

....

....

....

....

....

....

....

....

....

....

....

....

....

....

....

....

....

....

....

....

....

Exploring ethical issues

It is important to be able to assess the ethical issues involved in a scenario. Even though every scenario will be different, you should make sure you can apply your knowledge and understanding of animal welfare and ethics of animal management to identify all the possible ethical issues in a given situation.

Superpets sells a range of companion animals including rabbits and guinea pigs. It offers store credit for animals that are brought by the public for resale, even if they are a result of overbreeding or accidental breeding. Recently, Superpets has taken ownership of a single African grey parrot which is kept close to the cash desk to attract customers, but is not for resale. Superpets has also purchased a range of young reptiles to sell from an unknown breeder (including bearded dragons, blue-tongue skinks and royal pythons). Superpets has not received any details about their history.

Explore the ethical issues presented in this scenario.

Planning your answer

This is a long-answer question so you should spend some time planning your approach to ensure that you cover all the key points in a structured and coherent way. The example given below is one way to approach it. Look at this carefully and in the lines below, create your own plan or expand on the one given for this question.

- Introduction: outline different issues presented.
- Issue 1: adopting animals from the public. Explore problems such as introduction of diseases or parasites, lack of accurate information about history or where animals came from, offering store credit can encourage unethical breeding or stealing.
- Issue 2: store has accepted for sale animals from unknown breeder with no history. Consider questions around lack of information about health or breeding issues, offering animals for sale to public without knowing the history, were they caught in the wild?
- Issue 3: social species kept singularly. African parrot is social species. Explore issues around behaviour if parrot bonds with one person and could develop stereotypical behaviours. Being housed in busy shop unlike natural environment, could develop stereotypical behaviours, consider acceptable welfare standards including whether practices are morally acceptable.

....

....

....

....

....

....

....

....

....

....

....

....

....

....

Writing your answer

Now you have created a plan for an answer to the question, your next step is to complete the example answer below.

A good way to structure an answer to this type of question is for each issue, to first describe the issue and then to explore it further. Think about whether each aspect of the scenario is acceptable in terms of animal welfare, whether it is 'right', and whether there are further issues that could arise.

Superpets allowing the public to donate animals poses a problem because an animal's history may not be known. This information should be available because the animal will be put up for adoption and sold to the public. Not knowing its history means the animal cannot have a thorough health assessment, for example the animal may look healthy but possess a disease that is currently in its incubation period.

Another concern is ....

....

....

....

....

....

....

....

....

....

....

....

....

....

....

....

....

....

....

....

....

....

You will need to give more detail to analyse and explain further implications of the scenario. Consider how animals not indigenous to the UK may be bred or captured for the pet industry.

Remember to fully explain the implications by linking them to welfare issues that the animals may experience while at the pet store.

Non-indigenous species, such as the bearded dragon or royal python, may be bred from a reputable breeder, but they may also be caught in the wild and shipped to the UK. Considering Superpets has not been supplied with any information about the animals, the animals they have been given could be wild. Ethical issues that surround this scenario are that wild animals would have been subjected to severely stressful situations during their capture and transportation. Generally, this is unethical as neither welfare nor legislative requirements are being met.

Further problems can arise if the wild animals carry diseases that can be passed on to ....

....

....

....

....

....

....

....

....

....

....

....

....

....

....

....

....

....

....

....

....

....

....

....

You could continue to explore implications of keeping social animals in isolation. Ensure you link your answers to the scenario, for example by discussing the lone African grey parrot. It would also be useful to reference specific legislation that may not have been followed.

....

....

....

....

....

....

....

....

....

....

....

....

....

....

....

....

....

....

....

....

....

....

....

Links There is more information about legislation on pages 137–148 of the Revision Guide.

END OF REVISION TASK

Revision task 2

 You can now plan, research and undertake Revision task 2 with less guidance than in Revision task 1. You should use the skills you have been practising and there are some hints to help you. You will need to carefully read the Task Brief and Task Information and make a plan for how you would approach the research. You can then use your own research to make some notes on each of the areas indicated in the task information:

- legislative requirements
- welfare issues
- ethical issues.

The scenario in this example concerns a day care crèche for dogs. You must read both the brief and the documents within the stimulus material provided and consider what research you should complete.

Task brief

You are required to carry out research into the scenario provided in the task information below. You should consider the following areas in relation to the scenario:
- legislation and regulations relating to the animal species
- policies and practices relating to the setting and linkages to the welfare requirements of that species
- ethical issues relating to ownership of the species.

Task information

Top Dog Day Care is a new day care centre for dogs. It recently opened to allow clients to bring dogs into the centre to be looked after during the day and to be socialised with other dogs.

You work for the council and have been asked to carry out an appraisal with recommendations for Top Dog Day Care.

You may want to use visual aspects in your notes such as spider diagrams, tables or bullet points – this would be a good way of showing this information concisely.

Remember to use suitable headings in your notes. Using headings wisely will easily direct you to relevant legislation, or outline possible welfare issues. It may also be a good idea to note-take effectively by using bullet points, mind-maps and tables. You may find it useful to include images or sketches, if appropriate.

Always remember to include summaries to help remind you of the main aspects required.

 See page 152 of the Revision Guide for more information on appraisals. and pages 137 and 139 for information relating to the Animal Welfare Act 2006.

Remember businesses may need to adhere to several legislations and different regulations. You may need to refer to two or three legislations and these could also apply to visitors and colleagues as well as the animals. Be sure to check and research all relevant laws.

....
....
....
....
....
....
....
....
....
....
....
....
....
....
....
....
....
....
....
....
....
....
....
....
....
....

Now consider the policies and practices relating to the setting and welfare requirements of the dogs in the task information. It may be a good idea to think of the animals needs and how these are or are not met within the animal's environment on a day to day basis.

....
....
....
....
....
....
....
....
....
....
....
....
....
....
....
....
....
....
....
....
....
....
....
....
....
....
....
....
....

You need to consider ethical issues in the Task Information given and make notes on any relevant moral issue where you may be able to link to existing theories that may apply to a given situation. This should be relevant to the subject provided rather than individual opinions.

....
....
....
....
....
....
....
....
....
....
....
....
....
....
....
....
....
....
....
....
....
....
....
....
....

Stimulus material

For this revision task you are given a set of stimulus material that contains extra information that you will need to answer the activities in the revision task. Before you start working on your task, you need to carefully read through the stimulus material, taking note of what information is there. It's a good idea to make notes directly onto the stimulus material about what information might be missing or where information is incomplete.

The following stimulus material has been collected for you:
- Top Dog Day Care staff procedures when booking-in dogs
- Top Dog Day Care client form
- Top Dog Day Care layout
- Top Dog Day Care fire precautions
- Top Dog Day Care behaviour assessments.

Top Dog Day Care staff procedures when booking-in dogs

All staff must be fully aware of the booking in procedure and be trained appropriately.

- Gather client form and reconfirm all details.
- Check suitability of dog for day care by ensuring this is correctly marked as 'YES' on the booking form.
- Request any health concerns – dogs with major health concerns should not be accepted into day care.
- Clearly mark on the electronic diary that the dog has arrived.
- Note down any minor health concerns in the 'Notes' section in the electronic diary.
- Take payment for the day, or check status if 'block paid'.
- Take dog from owner in the booking area. Ensure owner leaves before entering.
- Take dog into play area.
- Use double gate system and ensure all gates are locked.
- Observe dog for 5 minutes.
- Secure dog's belongings in relevant area.

Top Dog Day Care client form

- This information is collected before dogs come into the centre for their first day at day care. This form can be completed with the client in the centre, over the phone or via email.

- Once the client form has been completed and deemed suitable to attend day care, provisions can be made.

- All forms must be kept in the database.

Name of dog:	
Breed:	
Description of dog (distinguishing features)	

Name of owner:	
Address:	
Telephone:	
Email address:	
Emergency contact name:	
Emergency contact telephone:	

Suitable for day care: YES ☐   NO ☐

Signed: _____

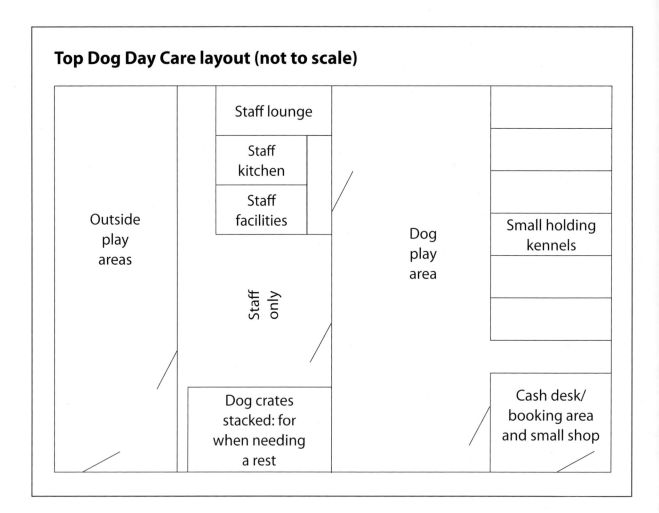

Top Dog Day Care layout (not to scale)

Outside play areas

Staff lounge

Staff kitchen

Staff facilities

Staff only

Dog crates stacked: for when needing a rest

Dog play area

Small holding kennels

Cash desk/ booking area and small shop

Top Dog Day Care fire precautions

This information is displayed on the health and safety notice board found in the staff-only area, and is also detailed in the staff handbook.

- If you notice a fire, raise the alarm by shouting 'fire' and alerting other staff members, or clients on site.

- Direct all clients and staff to the designated evacuation points at the other side of the customer car park.

- Do not put yourself or others in danger.

- People first: attempts to evacuate all customers and staff should be made before considering evacuating dogs.

- Where possible, dogs should be safely evacuated to the designated emergency area as quickly as possible. Leads can be found on hooks next to the emergency exit – once people have been evacuated and it is safe to evacuate dogs, staff should use these leads to remove the dogs and secure them appropriately.

- Fire extinguishers and fire blankets are provided in designated areas of the store. You should only use a fire extinguisher or blanket if you have completed fire safety training.

- Only attempt to put out a fire or rescue animals if it is safe to do so.

NB: Fire precautions are not listed in a specific order of events.

Top Dog Day Care behaviour assessments

All dogs entering the premises must have undergone a behaviour assessment to help identify whether the dog is suited to a day care or dog crèche setting.

The information produced from the behaviour assessment should be recorded on the client form so that it is obvious to all staff whether the dogs have 'passed' or 'failed' their behaviour assessment.

Behaviour assessments will include:

- Food test
  - Food should include small dog treats as well as bones.
- Reactivity test to toys
  - 'Squeaky' and 'non-squeaky' toys should be encouraged.
- Reactivity test to other dogs
- Reactivity test to people other than owners
- Spending a certain amount of time in a crate
- Spending a certain amount of time in a small day care kennel
- Undergoing handling and health checks
- Undergoing pressure test.

To answer the revision activities you will have carefully read through the task brief, carried out your initial research into the subject and thoroughly read through the stimulus materials provided.

In your actual assessment:
- The task brief and stimulus materials will be new each year and the secondary research sources you will need to find to relate to it will change.
- You may not be allowed to use your preparatory notes, or there may be restrictions on the length and type of preparatory notes that are allowed. Check with your tutor or look at the latest Sample Assessment Material on the Pearson website for details.

Writing an appraisal report

Write an appraisal report of Top Dog Day Care. Using the additional information provided, you should address:
- How Top Dog Day Care meets its legislation and regulation requirements for animal welfare when keeping dogs in a day care setting
- How Top Dog Day Care plans to meet the health and welfare needs of the animals in its care through their policies and procedures
- Ethical issues relating to the keeping the animals in this setting.

In order to write an appraisal report you will need to consider the information contained in the stimulus material as well as using your knowledge of animal welfare and ethics.

Firstly, consider legislation that must be adhered too – as with any species, the Animal Welfare Act (2006) must be addressed so ensure you comment on how well Top Dog Day Care does this, given the information available to you.

Next you could consider issues related to keeping dogs in smaller spaces, away from their home environment. For example:
- Have the dogs been habituated to this type of setting?
- What if the dogs have never left home? Would this be considered right or wrong?

In terms of focusing on health and welfare needs, use the information provided to consider whether the dogs' needs have been addressed. These could be:
- security
- safety
- consideration of 'quiet areas'
- consideration of injuries or illnesses
- disease prevention.

....
....
....
....
....
....
....
....
....
....
....

....

....

....

....

....

....

....

....

....

....

....

....

....

....

....

....

....

....

....

....

....

....

....

....

....

....

....

....

Links   For more information about relevant legislation, see page 141 of the Revision Guide.

Assessing the stimulus material

To what extent does the information provided in the stimulus material allow for a comprehensive appraisal to be conducted? In your answer, you must refer to any additional information you would need in order to complete a comprehensive appraisal report.

> To assess how comprehensive your appraisal can be given the information provided, you need to study each part of the stimulus material, and consider how it could be improved to get either more information or to clarify the facility's procedures.
>
> Think about the following:
> - Does the information provide staff with sufficient depth to carry out procedures or tasks well?
> - Do the procedures allow Top Dog Day Care to obtain sufficient important information from clients?
> - Is the documentation clear enough to allow you to understand whether legislation is being adhered too?
> - Is the documentation clear enough to ensure animal welfare requirements are being met?

....

....

....

....

....

....

....

....

....

....

....

....

....

....

....

....

....

....

....

....

....

Creating an action plan

Produce an action plan for Top Dog Day Care to address the issues identified in your appraisal. Your action plan must include:

- actions required by Top Dog Day Care management
- reasons for the actions
- timescales for the actions to be completed.

> Ensure you consider all aspects of the action plan, including how Top Dog Day Care can implement important missing information, and why these actions are important. Remember to be realistic with the timings of the actions.
>
> Three key areas are required when creating an action plan:
> - **Actions:** Think about what you highlighted about what is missing or could be improved. Also consider the order of priority in which actions need to be completed to ensure the pet store is ready for inspection.
> - **Why?** Explain why these actions need to be taken. This could be related to a current failure to meet legislative requirements or welfare needs, for example.
> - **Timescale:** Is there an expectation that actions are completed instantly, for example to address welfare issues, or can some be postponed to allow more urgent issues to take precedent?

....

....

....

....

....

....

....

....

....

....

....

....

....

....

....

....

....

....

....

 Links You can find more information about action plans in the Revision Guide on page 155.

Considering the ethical issues

The owner of Top Dog Day Care has decided to take in rescue animals in a separate part of the site. Top Dog Rescue Centre is located in the same building and uses the same entrances and emergency exits, but is located in an extension to the original premises.

A family has come into financial difficulties and has brought to the centre three rabbits, a litter of four four-week-old kittens and the family dog, a 12-year-old Labrador that appears to be overweight. They decided to keep the adult cat (the mother of the kittens) as she is fairly easy to look after, being quite feral.

Explore the ethical issues presented in the above scenario.

> This is a long-answer question, so spend some time planning what you might write about.
>
> Break the scenario down into the different key elements:
> - Location of animals – different species will be located together, or at least be able to see each other, which could cause high levels of stress. Animals could transfer diseases or parasites to existing animals, including the day care dogs.
> - Mammals should not be removed from their mother before being weaned at around eight weeks of age. This can pose not only health issues but also influence their behaviours in the long term.
> - Limited information has been given to the rescue centre about the animals' history, including health and breeding information.
> - Overfeeding animals and failing to provide correct exercise routines can cause health problems such as obesity.
>
> You could start your answer by analysing and explaining the implications of predator–prey species being kept so close together and the stress that may be caused to the animals. Then explore further issues. Remember to fully explain the implications you suggest by linking this to welfare issues the animals may experience.
>
> Consider the five needs of all the species involved.

> **Links** Revise this topic on pages 131–135 of the Revision Guide.

....

....

....

....

....

....

....

....

....

....

....

....

....

....

....
....
....
....
....
....
....
....
....
....
....
....
....
....
....
....
....
....
....
....
....
....
....
....
....
....
....

END OF REVISION TASK

Answers

Unit 1: Animal Breeding and Genetics

Revision task 1

Research

Breed	Standards
Dexter	Use: Meat and dairy Size: 300–400 kg Breeding: Extremely maternal, calving problems are rare. Heifers mature young and can be put to the bull at **15** to **18** months of age. Should breed regularly for **14** years or more. Temperament: Variable temperament but usually docile if handled regularly. Economics: Can be grazed on less acreage – more economical. High yield of **lean**, **tender** beef. Society website: www.dextercattle.co.uk
Aberdeen Angus	Use: Meat Size: **550–850** kg Breeding: Extremely maternal (good **surrogates**), calving problems are rare. Females calve easily and have good calf-rearing ability. Temperament: Good natured, **undemanding**, **easy to handle**. Economics: Hardy, adaptable, can be grazed on **less** acreage – **more** economical. High yield of marbled beef. Society website: www.aberdeen-angus.co.uk
Red Poll	Use: Meat Size: **550–850** kg Breeding: **Can be fertile until past their 12th year, maternal with a good milk yield.** Temperament: **Docile and easy to handle.** Economics: **Fatten readily, high quality beef.** Society website: http://www.redpoll.org
Limousin	Use: Meat Size: 650–1000 kg Breeding: High conception rate, calving problems are rare, good milking ability. Temperament: Can be volatile. Economics: Hardy, healthy, adaptable. Society website: www.limousin.co.uk
Hereford	Use: Meat Size: **800–1200** kg Breeding: **Fertility remains for many years with consistent calf birth weights, easy calving.** Temperament: **Docile and adaptable to different conditions.** Economics: **High quality beef.** Society website: www.herefordcattle.org

Husbandry requirements of cattle, page 5
Feeding**: depends on age, health, breed, weather, intended use, etc. The life stage of the animal will also play a big part in determining their nutritional requirements.**
Dehorning**:** before calves are **2 months old**, using a **hot** iron.
Castration: Castration is a permitted procedure in cattle (Mutilations (Permitted Procedures) (England) Regulations, 2007). Under the **Veterinary Surgeons Act** (1966) only a veterinary surgeon may castrate a calf which has reached the age of two months.
- Surgical: Anaesthetic must be administered in animals two months or more.
  Only **veterinary surgeons** are allowed to carry out this procedure.
- Rubber ring**:** Animal must not be more than **7** days of age.
- Burdizzo clamp: **Anaesthetic** must be administered in animals two months or more.
Weaning: **6–8 weeks, but is dependent on the calf eating sufficient concentrates (indicates the extent of rumen development).**
Worming: **as per manufacturer's instructions. Wormers may need to be effective against lungworm, roundworm, flukes, etc. Young cattle are most susceptible to worms.**
Vaccinations for beef cattle: **available for diseases such as chlostridial disease, leptospirosis, bluetongue virus, respiratory virus, salmonella.**

Mating behaviours of cattle, page 6
Mating strategy: in order to identify a suitable mate, cattle rely mostly on **visual (sight), olfactory (smell) and gustatory (taste)** information.
Mating season: **Cattle are polyoestrous with their cycle lasting approximately 21 days. Many farmers only allow cattle to mate within a short time frame (less than 60 days), so they only need to monitor the cattle closely within a short time frame.**
Mating behaviours (male): **Flehmen response; rubbing horns and grooming between the bull and cows is common.**

Controlling pregnancy in cattle, page 7
Physical: keeping bulls and cows/heifers separate.

Detecting pregnancy in cattle
Ultrasound scan: **invasive to get a clear image of the uterus.**
Hormone test: **non-invasive, can be tested through milk or urine in cattle.**

Nutritional requirements, page 8
Before gestation: **cows/heifers should have a body score of 5–6 for healthy calves. Feed should be changed to reflect the animal's need to gain weight post-lactation.**
During gestation: **gradual increase in nutrients during gestation.**
After gestation: **an increase in nutrients is needed to allow for lactation and health. This will then decrease as the calf begins to eat hard feed and forage.**

Research neonatal care strategies, page 9

Natural rearing system: calves are cared for maternally until weaning (which can occur anywhere **from 5 weeks to 10 months**).

Artificial rearing system: **calves are fed via a bottle or tube until weaning.**

By law (Welfare of Farmed Animals(England) Regulations 2007), calves must have received bovine colostrum within **the first 6 hours of life so it is important to check that the calves suckle within this period.**

Calves and cows should be observed **quietly from a distance and not handled unless necessary.**

Questions

> For long-answer questions you will be marked on the points you include in your answer and how well your answer is structured. These questions are marked below with a *. A good format to follow is to make a point, then back it up with evidence or examples. The key thing you need to get across to the person marking your assessment is that you understand the subject; things they may be looking for will include:
> - using terms correctly
> - discussing the number of points asked for
> - supporting each point you make
> - organising your answer.

1 (a)
Two survival strategies in cattle include their economic value as a source of food and resources and [one of the following] **their ability to utilise nutrients in roughage / the small number of predators in many countries**.

(b)
Any three of the following points explained: *
- condition of mouth/teeth/eyes being a desirable characteristic for breeding
- head shape/size makes birth easier and is a desirable characteristic
- markings/colour of skin/coat indicate the breed standard and are desirable characteristics
- size/condition of limbs indicate the health of the animal
- condition/formation of limbs/hooves/feet indicate the health of the animal, the breed standard, and desirable characteristics
- posture/conformation indicate the breed standard, the health, of the animal and their potential for injury
- anus/cloaca/genitals indicate their general and reproductive health
- previous breeding history indicates their health and suitability for use as a breeding animal
- horns indicate quality of previous handling, likelihood of maintaining health and safety of this animal and others, and their breed standard.

2 Limousin: generally hardy animals with a high conception rate and few breeding problems, making them suitable for the exposed conditions in the field. The fertility of the herd is indicated but only one calf is listed for sale. There is no mention of the health of the animals or their nature which could be an issue as Limousin can be volatile.

Dexter: need limited grazing due to their smaller size which would be beneficial on a smallholding. The breed is very maternal and heifers mature young so this herd could be ready to breed. They have been handled regularly which is beneficial for encouraging a good temperament.

Red Poll: fatten quickly and give high quality beef. They are hardy with a good temperament if handled regularly. The fertility of this herd is unproven and would need establishing to confirm their suitability for breeding. They have been handled regularly and are reported to have an easy temperament which would make them suitable starting animals for expanding into cattle farming. No information is provided on worming and vaccination status.

3 (a)

		Bull			
		Xb	Xb	Yb	Yb
Cow	XB	XXBb	XXBb	XYBb	XYBb
	XB	XXBb	XXBb	XYBb	XYBb
	Xb	XXbb	XXbb	XYbb	XYbb
	Xb	XXbb	XXbb	XYbb	XYbb

Phenotypic probability that these parents will produce a red heifer is: $\frac{1}{4}$

(b) Law of independent **assortment**, Law of **dominance**, Law of **segregation**

(c) DNA is passed from parents to their offspring; characteristics which are controlled by genes are therefore heritable. DNA can undergo mutations which can lead to variation in characteristics between animals. Some of these characteristics can confer an advantage to an animal, increasing its chances of survival and reproduction. Over time, these variations can lead to evolution.

4 (a)
Answer could include any four from the following: *
- growth rate of animals
- live birth rate
- oestrous cycle of species
- carcass yield
- market value
- suitable animals (genetics, temperament, health, conformation, breeding history).

(b)
- Selection intensity: a measure of how **superior** an animal is to **the rest of its herd/flock/group**.
- Selection response: a prediction of **how improved the offspring of a mating will be**.

(c) Your answer could include:
- Increased productivity increases food availability.
- Increased product yield improves commercial value.
- Increased efficiency gives a more cost-effective production.

(d)
Answers could include: *
- increased milk yield for greater productivity
- increased carcass weight for greater productivity
- rapid finishing for greater productivity
- increased hardiness for suitability in different conditions
- reduced dietary needs for reduced maintenance costs
- health for reduced maintenance costs
- high live birth rate for increased productivity
- good temperament for improved safety and ease of handling.

Your answer should conclude with a sentence summarising the relative importance of the factors listed.

5 (a) Visual signs such as non-return to oestrous and ultrasound scanning could be used to diagnose pregnancy in cattle.

(b) Hormone therapy is used in different ways in animal breeding. Firstly, hormone therapy can be used to synchronise oestrous so that AI or mating can be carried out within a short period of time. In addition, hormone therapy can be used to encourage superovulation which could increase the birth rate.

(c) The nutritional requirements of cows should be monitored by continually assessing the health of the animals, including body score, and the amounts of food consumed. During gestation cows need a gradual increase in nutrients to maintain their body condition. After giving birth, their nutritional requirements increase again to account for milk production. The amount of extra nutrients needed decreases during lactation as the calves begin to gain more nutrients from foraging.

(d)
The cow should be brought into a suitable shed or easy-to-monitor field prior to parturition. When the calf is born, ensure it is cleaned by its mother and breathing. The umbilical cord should be coated in iodine. The cow and calf should remain somewhere warm and dry.

Answer could also include: *
- Monitor regularly and check to see if the calf feeds.
- Health check calf (from a distance) and mother.
- Check placenta (if it is not eaten by the cow).
- Make sure field is not overstocked.
- Ensure sufficient water and food is available for all the animals.

6 (a)
Commercial – disadvantage: can be expensive to implement.
Social – advantage: disease resistance, development of new medicines.
Social – disadvantage: potential health risks to consumers.
Technological – advantage: technology is becoming more refined allowing for a greater scope of applications. *

(b)
Desirable traits can be encouraged, along with the expression of recessive genes.
There is also potential for reduced disease resistance.

(c)
Your answer could include discussion of any four from the following: *
- Animal welfare
  ◦ conditions in labs, unexpected impact on health
  ◦ improving health of individual animals and the breed
- Impact on non-modified animals
  ◦ modified genes could become widespread
  ◦ non-modified animals could be disadvantaged compared to modified animals
- Animal rights
  ◦ unethical to test on animals to develop the techniques
- Environmental impact
  ◦ modified animals could impact on the food chain – other animals could lose/gain resources
- Regulation
  ◦ potential difficulties selecting a regulatory body and ensuring regulations are adhered to
  ◦ developing and refining regulations will be time consuming
- Religious issues
  ◦ such as using genes from an "unclean" species in another and the impact this might have on an animal's suitability as food, etc.

The answer should include a conclusion that sums up the different issues.

Revision task 2

1 (a)
Mate recognition in dogs primarily relies on olfactory information. Animals give out pheromones which can remain in the atmosphere or on objects they touch for a long time. A female dog will release pheromones which indicate whether or not she is in oestrous. Dogs have the ability to move their nostrils independently to identify the direction of a potential mate. When approaching a potential mate, they may also use visual clues to determine if mating is possible.

(b)
Answers could include: *
- requirements of potential buyers
- time available
- space available
- selecting animals to breed depends on the health of those animals and the success of previous matings
- the ability to meet neonatal requirements.

(c) Dogs utilise a maternal neonatal care strategy. Each mother looks after their own pups.

(d) Prior to gestation, the bitch will need a healthy, high quality diet containing all the required nutrients. Within the first two weeks of gestation, the bitch's food should be gradually switched to a highly digestible food. For the first six weeks, there are no additional energy requirements, but after this 10% extra nutrients per week is required until whelping. During lactation, the bitch's nutritional needs can be 200–400% of the pre-pregnancy requirements, depending on litter size and health.

2 (a)
Answers could include any four of the following points: *
- health of the animal
- age of the animal
- lineage (genetics)
- temperament
- previous breeding history
- desirable characteristics.

(b) Lineage is known, so it is easy to identify any history of problems. This can be used to identify breeding animals which are likely to produce healthy puppies, improve the health of a breed and increase resistance to disease.

(c) Calculating the inbreeding coefficient will give an indication of how genetically similar the potential crosses are, which can help to identify the chance of each combination leading to inbreeding and the potential for recessive traits to be displayed. This in turn helps breeders to anticipate the extent of breed-related problems.

(d)
You could include any of the following points, giving a reason why it should be encouraged: *
- Being good with children is a requirement for a family animal.
- Being good around other animals for multiple pet households and ease of exercising in public places.
- Healthy and with good conformation to reduce the potential for veterinary treatment.
- Intelligent so they are easy to train.
- Good guard dog to protect the property.
- Hypoallergenic to increase their suitability for all households.
- Low maintenance: needs to fit with a busy family and potentially limited budget.

(e)
An example answer could be:
- Siberian huskies are considered to be very good around children due to their friendliness, intelligence and curiosity. However these traits make them unsuitable as guard dogs as they are more likely to view strangers as friends than suspicious or a threat.
- Springer spaniels are generally good with children and loyal, making them good watch dogs. They are not always aggressive enough to act as guard dogs.
- Kuvasz have been bred as guard dogs for centuries, however some can be aggressive, making them unsuitable around children.

3 (a)
Probability of blue eyes $= \frac{11}{39} = 0.28$

(b)
Answers could include: *
- Both dogs are young enough to breed from.
- Both have a positive temperament.
- Female 2 is a proven breeder; Female 1 is not.
- Female 1's ancestry is discussed; this information is not provided for Female 2.
- Conclusion could be that, given the little information provided, Female 1 might be suitable because of her lineage OR Female 2 might be suitable because of her proven breeding success.

(c)
Answers could include: *
- Ribs, spine and hip bones can be felt easily but are not visible.

- 'Waist' is visible.
- Small amount of fat can be felt under the skin.
- Abdominal tuck is present but not obvious.

4

Stud 1

		Stud 1			
		BE	Be	bE	be
Female	be	BbEe	Bbee	bbEe	bbee
	be	BbEe	Bbee	bbEe	bbee
	be	BbEe	Bbee	bbEe	bbee
	be	BbEe	Bbee	bbEe	bbee

Phenotypic probability $= \frac{1}{4}$

Stud 2

		Stud 2			
		BE	BE	bE	bE
Female	be	BbEe	BbEe	bbEe	bbEe
	be	BbEe	BbEe	bbEe	bbEe
	be	BbEe	BbEe	bbEe	bbEe
	be	BbEe	BbEe	bbEe	bbEe

Phenotypic probability $= \frac{1}{4}$

5 (a) Mutations in DNA lead to variations in DNA. Variations in DNA lead to differences in phenotypes and the characteristics of individuals.

(b) Neutral mutations have no effect on the organism. Harmful mutations can have a detrimental effect on the organism. Beneficial mutations give the organism an advantage.
Note: you could also discuss the impact each type of mutation has on biological fitness.

(c) Spontaneous mutations occur naturally and randomly, while induced mutations occur as the result of something in the environment, e.g. radiation or chemical damage.

(d) This is the result of a lethal allele. It cannot be bred out because heterozygous genotypes do not confer a disadvantage, which in this case is the hairlessness which is the breed standard.

6 (a)
Your answer should include the following points: *
- It can determine the sequence of genes
- This can then be compared with other animals
- It should identify any genes linked to the condition
- For example, sequenced genomes can be compared against genomes for healthy dogs and other dogs with the condition. Differences in the DNA sequence between healthy and symptomatic dogs can be identified and the defective DNA identified.

(b) The gene to be altered is identified then separated from the rest of the DNA. The target gene is then amplified and attached to a promoter, terminator and marker – these form the construct. This is inserted into the cells it is to be added to, and then the marker gene used to identify which cells have taken up the construct.

(c)
Your answer could include the following points: *
Advantages
- desirable characteristics can be continued
- economic gain.
Disadvantages
- expensive
- long-term effects not known
- potential reduced lifespan of the clone
- large scale cloning will reduce the gene pool.

Unit 2: Animal Biology
Revision test 1

1 (a) 0.23 ng/ml (1)
(b) 4.8 ng/ml (1)

2 (a) A = centriole (1)
B = cytoplasm (1)
C = mitochondria (1)
D = endoplasmic reticulum (ER) (1)
E = nucleus (1)

(b) The plasma membrane **controls** what can **enter** and leave the cell (1). It also allows cells to **adhere** to each other (1) and **communicate** with each other (1).

(c) The two fibres associated with muscle contraction are actin (1) **and myosin** (1).

(d) During muscle contraction, the two fibres **slide past each other** (1) **to shorten or lengthen the muscle** (1).

3 (a) Possible answers could include four of:
- osmosis
- endocytosis
- diffusion
- facilitated diffusion
- exocytosis
- pinocytosis. (4)

(b) Active transport requires **energy** (1) to move materials against a **concentration gradient** (1), from a region of **low to high** concentration (1) across a **semi-permeable membrane** (1).

4 (a) Possible answers could include three of:
- give birth to live young
- produce milk to nourish their young
- endothermic
- keratinised skin covering
- have three inner ear bones. (3)

(b)

Kingdom	**Animalia**
Phylum	**Chordata**
Class	Mammalia
Order	Pholidota
Family	Manidae
Genus	*Manis*
Species	*temminckii*

(4)

(c) odour molecules / chemicals in the air (1)

5 (a) Advantages of a double circulatory system are that there is more **blood flow** to tissues due to higher **blood pressure** (1). It also keeps **oxygenated and deoxygenated blood** separate (1).

(b) A = right atrium (1)
B = aorta (1)
C = left ventricle (1)
D = septum (1)

(c) Contraction begins at **the sinoatrial node** (1) which generates an **electrical signal** (1) that spreads through the right **atrium** then the **left atrium** (1). This forces the atria to **contract** and blood from the atria is forced into the **ventricles** (1). The impulse reaches the **atrioventricular node** (1) then travels through the **bundle of His** (1) which consists of **Purkinje cells** (1). It then goes around the base of the **ventricles** (1) where it causes the **ventricles to contract**.

(d) decrease in blood oxygen levels (1), increase in blood carbon dioxide levels (1)

(e) Possible answers could include:
Cause, one of: heart defect, valve problem, hole in the heart (1)
Symptoms, two of: coughing, weakness, exercise intolerance, cyanotic mucous membranes (2)

6 (a) 37–40 °C (1)

(b) The animal is able to maintain its own body temperature independent of the environment. (1)

(c) Receptors in the **thermoregulatory centre of the brain** (1) constantly monitor the **internal** body temperature (1). When they detect a decrease in body temperature, they **send signals to the brain instructing changes to** (1) increase the body temperature such as by **piloerection, vasoconstriction** or shivering (2). When the receptors detect that the body temperature has **increased** to within **the normal parameters** (1), they instruct the response mechanisms to **be deactivated** (1), via a **negative feedback** loop (1). [Or opposite]

7 (a) Mechanical digestion is where food is broken down physically. (1) An example of this is chewing [or other correct example]. (1) Chemical digestion is where food is broken down chemically. (1) An example of this is the role of enzymes [or other correct example]. (1)

(b) peristalsis

(c) In a ruminant, the stomach has four chambers (1). These are the **rumen, reticulum, omasum and abomasum**. Also in a ruminant, the cecum is **large** (1).

(d) Microbes help to digest **food in the rumen (1)** and are a source of **nutrients** (1).

8 (a)

Thymine	**Adenine**
Cytosine	**Guanine**

(b) Possible answers could include: brittle bones and teeth, long healing time for breaks or fractures, loose joints, weak muscles, hearing loss. (2)

9 Blood enters the **nephrons** under high pressure. This forces small molecules such as **glucose, urea, water** and **ions** out of the capillary and into the **nephron tubule**. Large molecules such as **blood proteins** remain in the blood. In the proximal **convoluted tubule** glucose, **amino acids** and some ions are **actively transported** back into the blood, then in the **Loop of Henle** water is absorbed through **osmosis**. In the **distal convoluted tubule**, the balance of ions is finely adjusted. Molecules which are not reabsorbed travel to the **bladder**. (8)

Revision test 2

1 (a) A = mandible (1), B = ulna (1), C = femur (1)

(b) Any four of the following: blood cell production, mineral storage, protection of internal organs, movement, shape, structure. Hearing may also be accepted. (4)

(c) A possible answer could be:
Birds have hollow bones (bones with air pockets) (1), which gives them less weight than the bones of land-bound animals. (1) They also have more fused bones (1), which also reduces their weight (1).

2 cervical vertebrae (1), coccygeal vertebrae (1)

3 Possible answers could include:
Forward-facing eyes: binocular vision for better depth perception (1), but reduced peripheral vision (1) for detecting movement to the side or behind (1).
Side-facing eyes: poor depth perception due to little overlap in visual range from each eye (1), but increased peripheral vision (1) to detect movement to the side or behind (1).

4 (a) i. **Protein:** builds tissues, repairs damage, forms enzymes and hormones (1 mark for any).
ii. **Lipids:** supply and store energy, insulates, supports and cushions organs, hormone formation, nerve conduction, absorption of fat soluble vitamins (1 mark for any).
iii. **Carbohydrates:** supply and store energy (1 mark).

(b) Possible answers could include: villi increase the surface area (1) of the intestines so there is more room for nutrient uptake to occur (1). Villi have a rich blood supply (1) to transport the nutrients taken up around the body (1), and encourage nutrients to diffuse into the blood quickly (1). Villi contain protein channels to encourage the uptake of nutrients via facilitated diffusion and active transport (1).

(c) Gassy bloat (1) occurs when the oesophagus is blocked (1). Frothy bloat (1) occurs when foam forms on top of the rumen liquid, stopping the escape of gas (1).

5 A = iris (1)
B = pupil (1)
C = cornea (1)
D = lens (1)
E = sclera (1)
F = choroid (1)

6 (a)

Part of cell	Function
Nucleolus	**Ribosome production** (1)
Ribosome (1)	Synthesise proteins
Golgi apparatus	**Packaging, secretion and storage of cell products** (1)
Mitochondria	**Respiration** (1)
Plasma membrane (1)	Regulate what enters and leaves the cell. This also allows the cell to communicate with other cells
Cytoskeleton	**Moves organelles, separates cells during division** (1)

(b) Rough endoplasmic reticulum (1): protein storage and production (1).
Smooth endoplasmic reticulum (1): lipid storage and production (1).

7 (a) 0.0007 mm or 0.7 micrometers µm (2 marks for correct answer with unit and working; 1 mark for numbers into formula, 1 mark if answer correct but no working is shown).

(b) single layer (1), nuclei at different levels (1)

(c) Simple columnar: has one layer and consists of column shaped (1) cells.
Stratified squamous: has two or more layers of flattened (1) cells.

(d) A group of specialised cells (1) working together (1) to carry out a particular function.

8 (a) A is receptor (1)
B is sensory neuron (1)
C is motor neuron (1)
D is effector (1)

(b) Stimulus detected by receptor (1), sensory neuron transmits impulse to the relay neuron in the CNS (1), relay neuron transmits impulse to the motor neuron (1), motor neuron transmits impulse to the effector (muscle) to produce a response (1).

(c) Calcium is released from neurons (1) and travels across synapses to initiate an action potential in neighbouring neuron (1).

(d) Propagation of action potentials along myelinated neurons (1) where depolarisation jumps from one Node of Ranvier to another (1).

9 (a) Answer can include two of: comparison of DNA base sequences (1), comparison of amino acid sequences in proteins (1), cross reactivity of antigens and antibodies (1).

(b) Show (inferred) evolutionary relationships between different living organisms (1).

(c) genus, species (1)

(d) Variation (1) in DNA occur naturally between animals within a species. These variations can confer an advantage, a disadvantage or be neutral. Variations which give an animal an advantage (1) can increase its chance of survival (1). Animals more likely to survive are also more likely to reproduce (1) and pass their DNA onto their offspring (1). Offspring which inherit the DNA conferring an advantage are then more likely to survive and reproduce themselves (1). Over time, the genetic differences can become so great that the animals can no longer interbreed to produce fertile offspring (1). Speciation has occurred (1).

Unit 3: Animal Welfare and Ethics
Revision task 1
Five animal needs, page 57

Animal need	Interpretation	Species-specific example
Need for a suitable environment	All animals kept in a pet store should have a correct environment which would be like what they have in the wild.	Zebra Finches should be kept in a suitable aviary which includes perches, enough space, ventilation and is secure.
Need for a suitable **diet**	All animals kept in a pet store should have the correct diet – this includes both **food** provision, supplementation and **water**, supplied at appropriate intervals.	Bearded dragons should be supplied with **fruits** and vegetables, as well as live feed (**crickets and locusts** for example). They should be given appropriate supplements including vitamin D3 and **calcium**.
Need to be able to exhibit normal **behaviour** patterns	All animals kept in a pet store should have facilities to encourage **natural** behaviour, this could be in the form of enrichment and **housing** design.	Rodent species could be supplied with nesting material such as **shredded paper** or hay. They could also be given items to gnaw on such as **chew blocks**, **climbing** apparatus would also be appropriate such as ladders, swings and **ropes**.
Need to be housed with, or apart, from other **animals**	All animals kept in a pet store should have the correct social structure, such as they would in the wild. This includes whether they are **solitary** (live alone) or **social** (group living) species.	Rodents can be both solitary and group living. Syrian hamster: **Solitary** animal that should be housed **alone when mature** as **they can fight**. Rats: **Social species that should be housed in small groups**.
Need to be protected from pain, suffering, injury and disease	**All animals kept in a pet store should have the correct health care provided as well as a life as free from stress as possible.**	Rabbits should be **vaccinated** at appropriate ages, as well as be provided with regular wormers and **flea** treatments. **Accommodation** should remain safe and secure at all times, so public **cannot access this**. If rabbits fight they should be **separated** where appropriate.

The correct environment for exotic species, page 58

It can be hard to replicate natural environments, particularly size – many captive animals need much more space than we can allow.
Key aspects of suitable environment
- Size/space – all dimensions need to be considered. Animals will use **height** as well as **width** and **breadth**. Animals may climb, swing, fly, swim or travel long distances which cannot always be provided in captivity.
- Enrichment – can natural environments be recreated? Generally, they can be hard to create, and in captivity we often use artificial structures and **toys** e.g. plastic hides and treat balls. Hygiene issues accompany natural enrichment like trees, logs, pools and rocks when it comes to disease control (they are harder to **disinfect** and remove etc.).
- Temperature and ventilation – some species require

environments that may be harder to recreate, e.g. **polar and desert climates**. It can be hard to provide wild environments in countries that do not experience similar weather, e.g. keeping Australia's native species in the UK requires certain equipment (bulbs, heat mats etc.).
- Light/dark cycles – it is natural for animals to have light and dark cycles. Their behaviour and feeding patterns may rely on this. Artificial lights in some enclosures are not always ideal, particularly if bulbs do not emit **ultraviolet rays**.
- Using equipment and barriers – some can be unsuitable for species, e.g. wooden barriers may not be ideal for animals that may **gnaw or chew**. Similarly, there are issues relating to using some types of equipment such as **heating elements**. Using heat mats and bulbs for reptiles can be detrimental to health, because **they can wrap around them so that they cannot move even if they become burnt**.

Behaviour of animals in captivity, page 59

Examples of stereotypical behaviour	Example species	Causes of stereotypical behaviour
Bar biting – animals will constantly gnaw or chew at the bars of their enclosure.	Pigs **Rats**	It is usually caused by an animal's environment. Here are some examples of where issues can arise: Lack of size and space – some animals travel miles each day in a container, or need to frequently have new areas to explore. Little **enrichment** – lack of stimulation is provided in general, and new stimulation is not given regularly. Interactions – many species need to socialise and smaller environments do not allow for this. Natural **environments** – artificial environments are often provided. Feeding – food is given to the animals rather than them **foraging** or hunting it as they would naturally.
Feather plucking – birds can self-harm by using their beak to painfully remove feathers.	Birds, particularly parrot species such as African Grey Parrots	
Weaving and head bobbing – animals will repeatedly move their heads from side to side (weaving) or up and down (head bobbing).	**Bearded dragons**	
Over grooming – animal will constantly lick and nibble their fur or skin, causing irritation, redness, and sometimes broken skin.	Dogs **Rodents**	

Other general points you could note include:

Keeping animals in a captive environment can be problematic when looking at unnatural behaviours. These have specifically been caused as they cannot access the environment that they should. Some people would therefore agree keeping animals in captivity is wrong. Captivity can in fact be managed, and providing animals with larger areas, using space wisely e.g. adding different levels or height, providing stimulation such as a range of enrichments can reduce stress levels and promote a repertoire of natural behaviours.

Bearded dragons, pages 60–61

Live feed: depends on size and age of the bearded dragon, e.g. adults can eat mealworms, waxworms, locusts and crickets.

Calcium and vitamin D3: important for the lizard's bone strength and development. They can easily develop metabolic bone disease if not provided with the correct vitamins and minerals.

Diet

Fruit and vegetables: e.g. carrots, cabbage, parsnips and kale, apples, strawberries, pears and melon.

Water: **can be obtained from the bearded dragon's diet: fruits and vegetables have a high water content, water bowls can also be provided as they may also like to bathe in this.**

External factors:

- Temperature is important for bearded dragons as they come from a hot climate.
- An area should be provided to obtain maximum temperature with a gradient that allows them to cool down if they need to.
- The hottest temperature is usually around **40** degrees Celsius, where the cooler end is around **28** degrees Celsius (usually a range to account for different ages).
- Not only does the bearded dragon require a light for heat, but also to absorb **ultraviolet rays** as it is likely to have little access to the Sun, unlike in the wild.
- Ventilation is important to ensure a flow of fresh air.

Enrichment:

Creating an environment where they have similar substrate to their wild environment is beneficial. Sand, or similar material, is good for burrowing and performing natural behaviours, but need to avoid ingesting (leading to **gut impaction**).

Reptile carpets also give the appearance of a natural environment, e.g. grassy or desert habitats. Objects that would be found in the wild, such as rocks, logs and pebbles, are good for **basking** and should be placed in the correct areas of the accommodation.

Food is also a good method of enrichment, as **live food** can be provided to the bearded dragons so that they can chase and catch their prey.

Accommodation materials

Material	Advantages	Disadvantages
Glass	Easy to clean Can visually check lizard without too much disturbance Holds heat well	Heavy **Can be expensive** Need to take care that lizard isn't burnt on hot glass
Plastic	Light and easy to **manoeuvre**	Usually smaller accommodation, so more suited to younger bearded dragons such as those only a few months old Does not hold **heat** as well as glass Not compatible with some heat sources
Wood	Aesthetically pleasing Useful when housing several types of animals (solid walls so animals cannot see each other) Most heat sources can be used within	Can be heavy Care must be taken with heat and wood but there are options for installing heat lamps safely.

Guinea pigs, pages 61–62

Diet

Your notes should include:

- Vitamins and minerals – guinea pigs require Vitamin C and can obtain this from a variety of fruits and vegetables and their pellets/mix.
- Hay or grass – required for the digestive system to work properly, as well as help wear teeth down.
- Pellets/mix – provides all of the nutrients required, but must be accompanied by other foods too.
- Water – fresh clean water provided daily, which can help with waste elimination as well as other processes in the body.

Environment

Your notes should include:

- Indoor and outdoor areas, as well as shelters to provide places to hide from predators, threats or weather.
- Enrichment could include another guinea pig as they're sociable, as well as having different feeds such as hay or vegetables, and tunnels and chew toys.
- Different levels could provide exercise.

Accommodation materials

Your notes should include:

- Wooden hutches are commonly seen as they can be strong and sturdy, but an indoor and outdoor area should be provided.
- A run can be attached.
- Sawdust or shavings can be used as a bedding material as well as straw; fresh hay is provided daily, but usually as food rather than bedding.
- Plastics can be used, but must be monitored for sharp edges as the animals may gnaw them; cardboard is also suited in the accommodation in the form of enrichment, but again must be monitored.

Other animals, page 63.

Your notes should refer to the welfare requirements for other types of pet species, focussing on diet, environment and accommodation needs.

General practices, page 64

Species	Cleaning routine	Accommodation checks
Rat	Spot clean – daily (except on days where full clean/disinfect may be completed) to remove old pellets, food and waste material such as soiled shavings. Full clean – once per week to remove all shavings, nesting material and enrichment and replace. Disinfect – once per week (same as full clean but disinfect before replacing clean shavings and enrichment).	Check locks/latch morning and evening. Check safety of enrichment particularly where plastic can be gnawed. Check condition of bars, to ensure they are not sharp and that animals cannot escape
Corn snake	Spot clean – **daily (except on days where full clean/disinfect may be completed)** to remove **waste material** such as soiled lining paper or substrate. Full clean – **once per week** to remove and replace all substrate e.g. paper. Disinfect – **every other week** (same as full clean, but disinfect before replacing clean paper and enrichment).	Check locks/latch **morning and evening**. Check condition of **enrichment**. Check condition of vivarium to ensure it is safe and **animals cannot escape**. Check **temperature** and heat source (not exposed or broken).
Budgie	Spot clean – daily (except on days where full clean/disinfect may be completed) to remove old seed and waste material such as soiled paper or lining. Full clean – once per week to remove and replace all shavings, nesting material and enrichment. Disinfect – once per week (same as full clean, but disinfect before replacing clean shavings and enrichment).	Check locks/latch in the morning and evening. Check safety of perches and other enrichment devices, as well as nest boxes. Check condition of bars to ensure they are not sharp and that animals cannot escape.
Bearded dragon	Spot clean – **daily (except on days where full clean/disinfect may be completed)** to remove waste material such as soiled **sand (or substrate) and leftover food including live feed.** Full clean – **once per week to remove and replace all substrate, e.g. sand.** Disinfect – **every other week (same as full clean, but disinfect before replacing clean sand and enrichment).**	**Check locks/latch morning and evening.** **Check condition of enrichment.** Check condition of vivarium to ensure **it is safe and animals cannot escape.** Check temperature and **heat source (not exposed or broken).**

Ethics, pages 65–66

Who are the stakeholders when considering opening up a pet store and how may this influence an ethical matrix?

	Health and welfare	Freedom and choice	Fairness
Animals	Animal welfare and conservation	**Behavioural freedom**	Intrinsic value of animals
Pet owners/ customers	**Health and happiness**	Freedom of action	Compliance with legislation
Consumers	Good income and working conditions	Options based on information supplied	**Choice and availability of different pets**

Your additional notes could include the following points:
Animals may be cared for well in the pet environment, being provided with food, social groupings and shelter.
Pet owners can benefit from having increased happiness and health for example interacting with pets as well as with some species getting the benefit of exercise.
Consumers can be a range of different stakeholders, for example pet store owners can seek different breeders to obtain different animals offering a large choice of suitable pets to their customers. Breeders also have the opportunity and choice to breed or to not breed selected animals.

What may the different ethical theories include?
Your notes could include the following points:
Sentience-centred – keeping some pets may be seen as ethical (however how they are treated may change this). A sentient animal that is kept well would be ethical, for example keeping a dog and ensuring it is treated correctly (good food, shelter, exercise etc). On the other hand, keeping a sentient animal could be unethical as it may be hard to provide for the animal as it would be kept in a wild environment. Remember there are also varying opinions as to what animals are considered 'sentient'.

Human-centred – humans are the focus in this ethical approach. With humans being number one it would be considered that keeping any animal including pets is ethical, regardless of what conditions are provided. Humans have no duty of care for other species and will always remain the priority. If somebody wanted to keep a pet, this is their entitlement to do so.
Environment-centred – this is the opposite of the human-centred theory. Environment-centred focuses on all animals and environments being equal, including humans. This means it could be interpreted that it is immoral to keep any animals as pets as we should help them thrive in their natural environment as well as protect their habitat.

Questions

*For longer answer questions you will be marked on the points you include in your answer and how well your answer is structured. These answers are marked with a * below. A good format to follow is to make a point, then back it up with evidence or examples. The key thing you need to get across to the person marking your assessment is that you understand the subject; things they may be looking for will include:
- using terms correctly
- discussing the number of points asked for
- supporting each point you make
- organising your answer.

*Writing an appraisal report, page 73

Health and welfare needs:
Consider how the animal's health and welfare has or has not been maintained.
Positives:
- Again animals are health checked before sale, as well as monitored for signs of good health specific to species (activity for example).
- **PPE is provided to reduce the risk of ill health and disease**
- **New animals to be quarantined before going on sale**

Negatives:
- Accommodation information does not provide depth (e.g. size)
- **Mammals appear to be located near the entrance**

Stimulus material to reference: **store layout plan, procedures when selling animals, animal health policy, animal accommodation requirements.**

Ethical issues related to animal welfare

Look at some of the information supplied by Superpets and provide a balanced overview of the ethical considerations:
- Animals are sentient beings and therefore should be provided with the correct environment and conditions – Superpets do a relatively good job at maintaining welfare such as **checking the animals as well as vaccinating the animals when necessary, making it ethical to keep these animals in this way. It is also only morally right to keep animals as pets if we do it correctly (maintaining the animals' needs, for example those detailed in the Animal Welfare Act 2006).**
- On the other hand, **keeping animals in enclosures that perhaps do not mimic natural environments (no discussion of enrichment or enclosure sizes, and groupings) would suggest that on welfare grounds it is unethical to keep these animals.**

Conclusion

Cover both plus and minus points, make clear which are the key issues:
- Evidence that legislation has been followed (e.g. ages of customers, ages of animals sold).
- Legislation, welfare, ethics all covered in some respects (e.g. accommodation needs, emergency procedures, reducing ill health).
- However, **some areas need more information to show that they have been considered, e.g. feeding information, enrichment.**
- Rank the issues discussed in terms of **their impact and which are the most urgent to address.**

Superpets has considered several aspects of the Pet Animals Act (1951) by providing a variety of procedures and documentation to its staff members. Firstly, there is clear evidence relating to the sale of the animals, both in terms of the animals' health and age of sale. All animals must be health checked before sale, checked twice a day before being on display to the public, and not sold until fully weaned for mammals (usually between 8–10 weeks). Superpets also refers to **the age and conditions of selling the animals; for example, customers must be 16 or above to be sold an animal, or 12 or over with suitable methods of consent.**

However, there is little evidence to suggest Superpets will provide suitable accommodation for the animals. **The documentation does not offer much species-specific information, which could therefore be open to interpretation. There is no reference to suitable sizes of accommodation or how many animals should be housed together due to the animal being a social or solitary species. This is also similar to the construction materials, temperature and humidity, for example. Essentially the information supplied is very basic yet essential.**

In relation to the Animal Welfare Act (2006), there is no mention of animals having access to **outside accommodation; therefore, all animals are likely to be accommodated indoors until they are rehomed, which could be for a considerable amount of time. All animals in a pet store would experience natural light and unlimited space if they were in the wild; however they may not if they are kept in a 'pet' or captive environment. Some animals need to receive ultraviolet rays from the Sun to remain healthy, and this therefore needs replicating in captivity. Superpets has not discussed replacing ultraviolet bulbs, or ensuring these are sold along with species that require them, for example for bearded dragons.**

*Assessing the stimulus material, page 78

In the guided answer, the student has discussed the Superpets staff procedures when selling animals. As well as this, your continued answer could include reference to the following:
- Some emergency and evacuation procedures are unclear or missing information, for example details as to who deals with the emergency, or who should be trained in this field. More specificity with what to do with the animals may also be required. There is also missing information with regards to the escape routes that must be taken in an emergency.
- Isolation and quarantine facilities are provided, but perhaps not in an ideal area (near staff kitchen) which could pose issues with zoonosis. A quieter area of the store may be better (but still out of customer access).
- There is no real detail of size and space provided for different species. Also location of some animals may not be ideal, e.g. mammals placed near a busy area of the store. Feeding, accommodation requirements and the health and cleaning schedules are all important aspects of the Pet Animals Act (1951).
- There is a set fire procedure which is a core aspect of the Pet Animals Act (1951), as well as being clear as to who is responsible for the pets in the store. The procedures are realistic, but perhaps could be clearer to ensure all staff are competent and happy with undertaking the procedures.
- Mammals are placed at the front of the store, which is a high traffic area. Some mammals may be stressed by this, as well as birds which are also closer to the front. However, the reptiles and mammals are kept at a good distance, which eliminates stress between predator and prey species.

*Creating an action plan, page 79

The guided answer for the action plan covers the need to provide more detailed species-specific accommodation information. Other areas you could cover are:
- **Action**: Store needs to clarify who to report to in the event of an emergency and which roles require this training.
- **Why**: This is basic yet key information which is directed by the Health and Safety at Work Act (1974).
- **Timescale/Urgency**: Urgent - to be completed before opening.
- **Action**: Reconsider the location of some species to be moved away from high traffic area.
- **Why**: Reduce stress levels of animals, for example mammals to be moved away from the till area/entrance, ensure predator and prey remain at a distance (e.g. keep small mammals away from the reptiles).
- **Timescale/urgency:** To be implemented and reviewed in time for store opening.
- **Action**: Relocate isolation and quarantine facilities, or highlight in the policies relevant procedures when using these.
- **Why**: To ensure it is clear, what is expected when using these, for example upon entry PPE is to be worn, and upon exit, PPE is to be placed in the yellow bins provided – this is to ensure the risk of disease is reduced.
- **Timescale/urgency:** To be implemented and reviewed in time for store opening.

*Exploring ethical issues, page 81

A lack of past history and encouragement of overbreeding have been considered in the guided answer. Other ethical issues you could explore that arise from the scenario include:
- Adopting animals from the public could include wild animals. If they are brought in with diseases, these could be passed on to healthy stock. They could even spread further if zoonotic, to new owners as well as staff and any pets or people they may also come into contact with. The groups of animals that are commonly known for breeding and brought in include mammals, birds and reptiles. Wild caught animals (for example reptiles) can be trapped and transported from other countries in very poor conditions. These animals often have a high mortality rate. This is due to lack of ventilation, space, no food, water or rest breaks, and generally unsanitary conditions.

- Social animals kept in solitary enclosures could develop stereotypical behaviour and cause high amounts of stress and self-mutilation, as well as pose other health issues. The African Grey Parrot is a social species that would live in social flocks and interact with other birds regularly. When putting into captivity (pet store environment) the bird could experience stressful situations, for example being crowded by customers, other animals coming into the pet store as well as different noise levels, including the telephone and cash register. This could present itself in stereotypical behaviour as a way of coping.
- Members of the public breeding animals for sale to Superpets may not have followed the relevant legislation (Pet Animals Act 1951, as well as Animal Welfare Act 2006).
- Accommodation requirements as well as natural behaviours are being limited in the parrot's accommodation. Issues with stress from the public too.

Planning your answer, page 81

Your plan could include the following points:

- Adopting animals from the public – animals could transfer diseases or parasites to animals that are already housed in the pet store. Offering cash equivalent to the public may also encourage overbreeding rather than deterring the behaviour.
- No information has been given to Superpets about the animals' history, such as any health or breeding issues, or where they have come from – whether they were caught in the wild, for example.
- Social species kept singularly – parrots can often bond with one person and can develop stereotypical behaviours easily if they are not housed correctly and allowed to express for their normal social behaviours.
- Another concern **is that allowing the public to bring animals in for donation may encourage overbreeding because breeders may assume that the pet store will take extra animals in. Breeders may also delay neutering the animals as they know that Superpets will arrange it when they receive the animals. Overbreeding in general terms is unethical as it may cause health issues such as genetic defects as well as discomfort if they have been bred for specific traits, for example large heads.**

Writing your answer, page 82

Using the information provided to you in the scenario you will need to explore each issue individually. You should record how the ethical issue can be perceived from several view points as well as making links to ethical theories. You should justify your answer by identifying any welfare issues that may arise from these issues. Adopting animals from the public is the first ethical matter presented. In continuing the guided answer, you could discuss the benefit to the animals being in this environment compared to being released into the wild or euthanized which could otherwise happen. On the other hand, animals could transfer diseases or parasites to animals that are already housed in the pet store. Combining this with offering cash equivalents to the public may also encourage over breeding rather than deterring the behaviour. Looking at the human centred theory compared to the environment centred theory would suggest that this is both ethical and unethical. Be sure to remain unbiased and give different opinions.

In the guided answer on page 83 the student has considered issues around no information having been given to Superpets about the animals' history, such as any health or breeding issues, or where they have come from, for example, whether they were caught in the wild. When continuing the answer, remember to structure your answer to review both ethical and unethical aspects. Discussing the consequentialism theories would allow you to justify both arguments with 'the right end justifies the actions'. The animals could suffer long term if they have underlying health issues, or were wild caught and have suffered throughout, a poor end for the animals making this unethical. On the other hand, the animals could live a full and healthy life and never have any issues, therefore it is morally acceptable.

On page 84, in exploring the implications of keeping social animals in isolation, consider that within the scenario it was evident that social species are being kept singularly. You could discuss that parrots can often bond with one person and can develop stereotypical behaviours easily if they are not housed correctly and allowed to express their normal social behaviours. In a pet store setting it would be hard to change this, but to consider both sides you could discuss the utilitarianism theory. It may be suggested that this is OK as for the most part, people will be happy as they are able to bond and socialise with this exotic interesting animal, regardless of the animal's welfare or rights (which thinking about deontological ethics would be the opposite). You could also comment on the stakeholders in this situation and consider an ethical matrix. Examples could include potential owners, the animals, pet store owners and breeders.

Revision task 2

*For longer answer questions you will be marked on the points you include in your answer and how well your answer is structured. These answers are marked with a * below. A good format to follow is to make a point, then back it up with evidence or examples. The key thing you need to get across to the person marking your assessment is that you understand the subject; things they may be looking for will include:
- using terms correctly
- discussing the number of points asked for
- supporting each point you make
- organising your answer.

*Writing an appraisal report, page 95

You will need to use the information provided in the stimulus material to write a comprehensive appraisal report that should look at each piece of material provided. To write a suitable report you should consider all three important aspects laid out to you, including legal, ethical and welfare considerations. When examining these three aspects you should be thinking about any legislations and policies that should be adhered to, whether the information is deemed right or wrong in terms of keeping the animals that has been presented in the given information, and ensure you solely focus on the scenario and the welfare issues that could be identified in this instance.

Your appraisal report should contain the following points. The key piece of legislation covering Top Dog Day Care provision is the Animal Welfare Act (2006). This requires that the dogs' needs are taken into consideration, e.g.

- **Somewhere suitable to live** – Accommodation requirements are considered having holding kennels, crates and the play area, however the sizes are not provided to ascertain how suitable these are for a prolonged time. Exercise facilities (toileting area) is also not obvious, however there is an outside area for the dogs. This information can be found in Top Dog Day Care lay out in the stimulus material.
- **Suitable diet** – There is no indication in the stimulus material as to whether the dogs will be provided with any food or water throughout their time at the day care centre.
- **Normal behaviours and housed with or without other animals** – Housing the dogs in a play area allows the dogs to play and socialise together, as well as being able to have time away from this area if they require this. This information can be found in Top Dog Day Care lay out in the stimulus material. There is no mention of habituating the dogs to this type of setting, e.g. leaving the dog at the centre for a trial period to check suitability. This information is missing from the stimulus material but would be suitable within the behaviour assessment.
- **Protection and treatment** – Only healthy dogs allowed to enter facility, as well as maintaining safety of the dogs throughout their stay, e.g. double gate system. The facility has considered 'quieter areas' away from the dogs playing, as well as kennelled areas. Giving the dogs time to rest, however could cause stress if

the dogs can still see each other. The facility will only take dogs that have had an assessment, which reduces the likelihood of injuries. There is no mention of vaccination details or whether animals may be taken to the vets if required. This information can be found in Top Dog Day Care staff procedures when booking-in dogs, Top Dog Day Care lay out and Top Dog Day Care behaviour assessments in the stimulus material.

The information supplied for legislative requirements also can be linked to the health and welfare needs of the dogs whilst in Top Dog Day Care's hands.

Ethical issues that could be detailed include:

- Keeping dogs in smaller spaces away from their home environment:
  - Because there has been no indication within the stimulus material as to the duration of stay in the smaller spaces (e.g. crates and small holding kennels), or sizes of these, you could argue this is suitable as well as unsuitable.
  - Suitable – smaller spaces are used to allow dogs to rest and have some quiet time away from the other dogs. Could be used for puppies or senior dogs that require more rest time. Being away from their home environment could be a good type of enrichment.
  - Unsuitable – keeping animals in smaller spaces for long periods of time can promote health issues as well as stereotypical behaviours. Stress could also be caused being away from their home environment, which again could lead to abnormal/stereotypical behaviours such as pacing the play area or self-mutilation.
- Have the dogs been habituated to this type of setting?
  - The stimulus material does not indicate that the dogs are habituated to this type of environment. This could be considered unethical as the dogs are not given the opportunity to get used to this setting which could again cause increased levels of stress for them. In the instance of stress, the dogs could again start to exhibit abnormal/stereotypical behaviour.

*Assessing the stimulus material, page 98

Your assessment of the extent to which the information provided in the stimulus material allows for a comprehensive appraisal should look at each piece of stimulus material and assess how complete it is, and whether more information is needed. Your answer should be clear and should aim to identify all areas where there is insufficient information and explain what additional information is needed and why. You need to make sure that your arguments take into account the specific stimulus material provided and be clear in your reasoning. Your answer could include the following points:

- **Staff procedures:** There are set procedures for the staff to follow, but there is no clear workflow or order given so it would be easy for a member of staff to miss out one of the items. There should be more depth to the procedure to allow staff to gather sufficient information when asking clients for details, as well as booking the dogs in to the facility as well as for the behaviour assessment: what needs to be provided? Staff are requested to check the dogs suitability for the day care setting and also ensure the area is secure. This can eliminate behaviour problems that could occur within the organisation, as well as ensure dogs do not escape.
- **Client form:** The form is basic. It does include emergency information which is essential when needing to contact the client. There is also information related to the identity of the dog. However, there is no indication of whether dogs have been checked for vaccination, e.g. records seen or copy attached. There are no records regarding behavioural needs of the dog, previous experience of day care or issues around experiences with other dogs. A signature is also required from staff to highlight suitability of the dog; however, the form is not particularly clear. There is also some important information missing from the forms that could be added. Information that will be required by the facility includes: age/gender/neutered or unneutered/vet information/vet treatment if required and owner cannot be contacted.

- **Legislation**: The information provided in the stimulus material is not linked to any legislation clearly, but there is clear guidance with regards to fire safety (found in the stimulus material within the Top Dog Day Care fire precautions) and security for the dogs (found in the stimulus material within Top Dog Day Care staff procedures when booking-in dogs) as well as detailed behaviour assessments carried out before taking them into the centre (found in the stimulus material Top Dog Day Care behaviour assessments). Stress free environments are not possible, but precautions made for quieter areas. These elements can form part of the Animal Welfare Act (2006), as well as the Health and Safety at Work Act (1974), like another business.
- **Day care layout:** The layout document of the facility is basic which does not indicate dimensions of specific depth. For example, which are fire doors, or where the double gate systems are located. The materials that make up the kennels and crates are also not detailed within the stimulus material Top Dog Day Care layout. There are no isolation facilities provided for dogs showing signs of illness, etc. It would be advisable to have this type of information to ensure animals are protected from illness, which is one of the five animal needs. It also will ensure anyone who observes the plans can be sure of how the facility can cater for the dogs' needs and meet the Animal Welfare Act (2006). The layout does incorporate an inside and outside area which is suitable to the dogs' needs on a day-to-day basis.
- **Fire precautions**: Procedures are provided for staff to follow and include information about what equipment is available. This is beneficial as staff can be trained to use these types of equipment. The information that is provided to staff with regards to the fire procedures is basic and no clear order is given, this could mean important aspects are missed. Within the set procedures there is a lack of contact information or who to report to in the event of an emergency, e.g. fire warden, and named contacts which is important for staff to be aware of in this scenario. There is also no information as to where the designated fire evacuation and assembly points are located. This is not included on the lay out either.
- **Behaviour assessments:** There is sufficient information about the types of behaviour assessments to be completed, which are suited to the organisation and are comprehensive, but no indication of how to complete the sub-tests. The stimulus material does not present any direct procedure and record form to be used within the behaviour assessment, which could be used to indicate whether the dog has been successful in the several areas outlined as well as important information discovered within the behaviour assessment. This should be then stored and kept with the client form, which can then be considered when necessary.
- **Daily routines:** The stimulus material does not contain any information or procure with regards to the day-to-day running of the facility to include information about taking dogs out of the play area on a lead outside, or time within crates or holding kennels.

When reviewing the stimulus material, you should look at each piece of information individually and evaluate them. It is useful to consider the positive aspects of each piece, as well as what is missing, therefore improvements can be suggested. For example, can staff complete procedures or obtain sufficient information from them? If this is not the case, what important elements are missing in order to obtain this information?

*Creating an action plan, page 101

Your action plan needs to have a comprehensive set of recommended actions which clearly address the issues you identified in the previous activity. For each action you need to explain clearly why it is recommended, you need to be clear about the priority of each action (is it urgent or not?) and apply realistic timescales to the actions, bearing in mind the scenario you have been given. It may take longer for an existing business to action things when they also have to run their business than it would for Top Dog Day Care in this case when they are only at the application stage. You don't need to use the layout given below as long as you are clear about what is being suggested, why, timescale and priority for each action.

- **Action**: Revise the set procedures to include a step-by-step approach or clear workflow for both the booking-in and fire procedures.
- **Reason**: In order to eliminate issues or problems during booking-in, or at times of emergency.
- **Priority**: Important, but not urgent.
- **Timescale**: In time for next review in 6 weeks' time.

- **Action**: Revise the client form to include more important information including: vaccinations, what to do in case of emergency and treatment needed. In addition, include basic important information, such as gender and age of the dog.
- **Reason**: To allow a more thorough assessment of the suitability of the dogs to the facility. For example, if necessary precautions have been made with regards to disease prevention from the owner, as well as to monitor an animal's health or status, e.g. allowing entire dogs into the facility or solely neutered dogs.
- **Priority**: Urgent.
- **Timescale**: In time for next review in 6 weeks' time.

- **Action**: Revise the documentation of the layout of the facility to highlight where isolation facilities will be located on the plan (this needs to be out of public areas, e.g. within the staff area) as well as more depth in terms of the type of doors or gate systems used.
- **Reason**: Dogs that show signs of illness should be moved away from the main area and where access to other dogs can be made. This will prevent the spread of any illness to other dogs, but also ensure the dogs can have time to rest and recuperate and be monitored by staff easily. Evacuation doors and double gate systems should be highlighted to staff and clients to ensure they know what procedures must be followed in specific locations.
- **Priority**: Urgent.
- **Timescale**: In time for next review in 6 weeks' time.

- **Action**: Clarify who to report to in the event of an emergency. This information should be supplied in the documentation, e.g. designated warden, and should also be available in staff areas (as suggested in the procedure). The designated evacuation and assembly points need to be detailed either on the lay out or with the fire procedure document.
- **Reason**: In order to make it clear for staff to know who to report an emergency to, or if they are unsure of a particular procedure, e.g. fire procedure. In addition, staff know where to go in the event of an emergency, as well as direct clients to a safe place.
- **Priority**: Important, not urgent.
- **Timescale**: In time for next review in 6 weeks' time.

- **Action**: Create a further procedure document to be used alongside the behaviour assessment procedure that will then be kept with the client form.
- **Reason**: The process for the behaviour assessments to be carried out will be evident to ensure no mistakes are made and the behaviour assessment is as stress free as possible, as well as the outcome of each sub-test being clear on the additional test form. This will clearly highlight if the dog has passed or failed each sub-test, as well as space to document any other findings during the assessment that may be important during assessment.
- **Priority**: Less urgent.
- **Timescale**: In time for next review in 6 weeks' time.

- **Action**: Create a further policy that incorporates the day-to-day running of the facility, to include information about taking dogs out of the play area on a lead outside, or time within crates or holding kennels.
- **Reason**: to ensure staff are aware of time scales to be housed within the different environments, as well as when to allow dogs time away from the play area when required. This could include information about what behaviours may be seen that may require time away from other dogs, e.g. constant mouthing or mounting, or for senior dogs and puppies that might require more rest. This should reduce stress levels and consider each dog's needs individually.
- **Priority**: Important but not urgent.
- **Timescale**: In time for next review in 6 weeks' time.

*Considering the ethical issues, page 104

A discussion of ethical issues will depend on the scenario you are given. Some points you could explore for the scenario given in this Workbook are given below, but you should expect to have to adapt your approach for different scenarios. You should always ensure that you explore different ethical viewpoints, that you give examples linked to the scenario presented to you, that you clearly structure your response in a logical order and make a judgement that is supported by the evidence given. For this scenario, you should consider the following points:

- **The location of the rescue animals** – Although the species will be kept in different areas, they are still relatively close and will be able to hear and smell each other. This could cause stress to the dogs coming in for day care, as well as those kept in the rescue centre. They will need to pass each other when using the same exits/entrances. Predators and prey should be kept at a great distance or in a completely separate area.
  - Ethical issues may arise since the animals are deprived of a natural environment as they cannot escape from humans or other animals, as well as this not being the 'norm' for housing these different animals. It could be argued that animals should remain in the wild and not be kept as pets. Although we have domesticated animals over many years, both wild and domestic animals can exhibit unnatural behaviours when kept in a captive environment, for example a dog or bear showing signs of self mutilation.
- **Litter of kittens from the family described** – Young mammals should remain with their mothers for as long as possible – the adult cat is still around and therefore could be brought in together or kept together until fully weaned. Early weaning can impact future development, as well as create stereotypical or behavioural problems, e.g. wool sucking. It may be suggested that the kittens should be brought in with the mother so the kittens can be fully weaned properly at around 8–10 weeks of age.
  - Ethical issues that may be seen is the scenario that there is insufficient care given to the kittens in the rescue centre compared to being kept with the mother. Overbreeding could also be a concern here where the mother is being bred and would be better to come to rescue too. It is also unethical to allow owners to keep pets if they are unable to care for them properly.
- **No history for some of the animals including the three rabbits and the family dog, aged 12** – Lack of history or knowledge of health or breeding issues could result in return to the rescue centre if managed to get re-homed which can create further behaviour problems for the animals, as well as cost involved to a charity, which means not being able to afford to help other sick or abandoned animals.
- Ethical issues that may arise are that the animals may have previously been kept in an inappropriate environment and have been used for overbreeding. Although companionship for the rabbits has been catered for, it is not clear whether the rabbits have been or should be kept together, or whether any of the animals has been treated for medical issues or vaccinated, etc. Again it may be considered to be unethical to treat animals in this manner. If animals that have not been vaccinated have access to the rescue animals, they could pass disease on easily, for example myxomatosis in rabbits.
- **Animals not taken in to the centre** – If the animals are not taken in by the rescue centre they may be further neglected, for example abandonment, or need to be euthanised by the owners. Ethical issues related to abandonment or euthanasia may be that all animals have the right to live and given the

opportunity to thrive. Abandonment can cause suffering, as the animals will not have access to their requirements, e.g. health care, food and accommodation, etc. It is unethical to allow an animal to suffer. Although euthanasia does not see any animal suffer, this could be deemed unethical as the animals are healthy and should be allowed to live a long and healthy life. The rabbit ages have not been provided, however the 12-year-old dog could still live a healthy life for another 5 years. The kittens are also very young, and could also live 20 years each.

- **Legislation not adhered to by owners that fail to exercise animals sufficiently or continually provide the incorrect diet** – This can be linked to the Animal Welfare Act (2006) and the animal needs not being sufficiently catered for. Lack of exercise accompanied with overfeeding animals can also cause behaviour issues, which again can make animals harder to re-home (for example, dogs that have been overfed and have picked up bad behaviours may not be able to be re-homed with children, as they may beg, steal and jump up, which could cause further issues).
- Ethical issues related to over-feeding and not exercising animals (generally causing morbid obesity) are present as the cause of these health issues have been created by human care (or lack of), and are not often seen in wild species. This can be seen as immoral.

When writing and reviewing your information, you should look at each element of the given scenario and consider both welfare and ethical implications that may arise. It is useful to also provide examples where you can to support the information you have discussed, as well as link these to different viewpoints. Justification should be evident throughout your answer, ensuring you use the correct terminology with a clear logical structure.

Notes

Notes

Notes

Notes